726 T

D1380886

efore

English Church Architecture

A VISUAL GUIDE

English Church

Architecture
A VISUAL GUIDE

Mark Child

B. T. Batsford Ltd London

First published 1981
© Mark Child 1981

Filmset in 10pt Palatino by
Elliott Bros. & Yeoman Ltd.

Printed by Elliott Bros. & Yeoman Ltd.,
Speke, Liverpool L24 9JL
for the Publishers B. T. Batsford Ltd
4 Fitzhardinge Street, London W1H 0AH
ISBN 0 7134 3762 6

Frontispiece: Long Melford, Suffolk,
from the south east

Contents

List of Illustrations 7

Acknowledgments 9

1 Anglo-Saxon 600–1066 *11*

2 Norman 1066–1160 and Transitional 1150–1200 *23*

3 Early English 1200–1300 *42*

4 Decorated 1300–1377 *56*

5 Perpendicular 1377–1547 *70*

6 Renaissance and Classical 1547–1830 *87*

7 Victorian 1830–1900 *102*

Index *115*

List of Illustrations

1 Greensted juxta Ongar, Essex: early eleventh-century nave
2 Worth, Sussex: view from the east
3 Wing, Buckinghamshire: polygonal Saxon apse
4 Bradwell juxta Mare, Essex
5 Monkwearmouth, Durham: the west porch and tower
6 Escomb, Durham: large blocks of stone in the exterior
7 Bradford on Avon, Wiltshire
8 Wareham, Dorset
9 Codford St Peter, Wiltshire: ecstatic figure on a ninth-century cross shaft
10 Inglesham, Wiltshire: Virgin and child
11 Bradford on Avon, Wiltshire: angels above the chancel opening
12 St Bene'ts, Cambridge: animal carving and impost
13 Deerhurst, Gloucestershire: animal head
14 Daglingworth, Gloucestershire: crucifixion
15 Barnak, Northamptonshire: seated Christ
16 Breedon-on-the-Hill, Leicestershire: sculpture of the Virgin
17 Winterbourne Steepleton, Dorset: flying angel
18 Early walling technique
19 Jarrow, Durham: section of seventh-century walling
20 Earls Barton, Northamptonshire: the tenth-century tower
21 Barton on Humber, Lincolnshire
22 Sompting, Sussex: the eleventh-century tower
23 Deerhurst, Gloucestershire: tower openings
24 Monkwearmouth, Durham: tower opening
25 Brixworth church, Northamptonshire, from the south
26 Barnak, Northamptonshire: impost
27 Netheravon, Wiltshire: Saxo-Norman capital
28 Escomb, Durham: doorway
29 Somerford Keynes, Gloucestershire: doorway
30 Bradford on Avon, Wiltshire: doorway
31 Repton, Derbyshire: the Saxon crypt
32 Potterne, Wiltshire: font
33 Plan of the original twelfth-century apsidal building
34 Hales, Norfolk: Saxo-Norman church
35 Fingest, Buckinghamshire: the tower
36 Tixover, Leicestershire: the tower
37 Barfreston, Kent
38 Kilpeck, Herefordshire, from the east
39 Stewkley, Buckinghamshire, from the north west
40 St Nicholas, New Romney, Kent: the tower
41 Iffley, Oxfordshire: the west front
42 St John's, Devizes, Wiltshire
43 Norman decorative mouldings and decoration
44 Highworth, Wiltshire: carving, probably tympanum
45 Old Shoreham, Sussex: the crossing tower
46 Colney St Andrew, Norfolk: the tower
47 Roughton St Mary, Norfolk
48 St Michael, Oxford
49 Kilpeck, Herefordshire: the south door
50 Tickencote, Rutland: the chancel arch
51 St John's, Devizes, Wiltshire: the Norman chancel
52 Melbourne, Derbyshire: piers of the nave arcade
53 Devizes, Wiltshire: Norman enrichment
54 Stapleford, Wiltshire: the nave arcade
55 Stanton Fitzwarren, Wiltshire: font
56 St Nicholas, Brighton: font
57 Climping, Sussex: the tower

58 Thirteenth-century additions to the ground plan
59 Inglesham, Wiltshire
60 Amesbury, Wiltshire
61 Uffington, Oxfordshire
62 Warmington, Northamptonshire: the spire
63 Church Knowle, Dorset: the west tower
64 Felmersham, Bedfordshire: the west front
65 West Walton, Norfolk: the tower
66 Bishops Cannings, Wiltshire
67 Long Sutton, Lincolnshire: one of the earliest lead spires
68 Early English windows
69 Ockham, Surrey, from the south east
70 West Walton, Norfolk: the nave arcade
71 West Walton, Norfolk: capital
72 Ivinghoe, Buckinghamshire: capital
73 Early English piscina and sedilia
74 The fourteenth-century contribution to the ground plan
75 Patrington, Yorkshire
76 Bishopstone, Wiltshire
77 Compton Beauchamp, Oxfordshire
78 Heckington, Lincolnshire, from the south west
79 Edington, Wiltshire
80 Whitbourne, Herefordshire
81 (a) Ball-flower (b) Four-leafed decoration
82 Patrington, Yorkshire: interior
83 Higham Ferrers, Northamptonshire: the east end
84 Leominster, Herefordshire
85 Leighton Bromswold, Huntingdonshire: the south door
86 Ogee-headed doorway
87 Decorated piers, arches and bases
88 Decorated piscina and sedilia
89 Brailes, Warwickshire: font

90 Ground plan showing early fifteenth-century extensions
91 The late fifteenth-century final transformation
92 St Cleer, Cornwall
93 Lanreath, Cornwall
94 Cullompton, Devon: the tower
95 Northleach, Gloucestershire
96 Long Melford, Suffolk: from the south east
97 Roofs
98 Needham Market, Suffolk: the roof
99 March, Cambridgeshire: the nave roof
100 Vaulting
101 Cullompton, Devon: the south chapel
102 Cricklade, Wiltshire: the tower
103 Taunton, Somerset: the tower
104 Ashburton, Devon: the west tower
105 Northleach, Gloucestershire: the south porch
106 Cirencester, Gloucestershire: the south porch
107 St Stephen's, Walbrook, City of London
108 Ingestre, Staffordshire
109 Willen, Buckinghamshire
110 Farley, Wiltshire
111 Frampton, Dorset
112 Portland, Dorset
113 Hardenhuish, Wiltshire
114 Blandford, Dorset
115 Gayhurst, Buckinghamshire
116 Moreton, Dorset
117 Glynde, Sussex
118 St Martin's in the Fields, London
119 Mildenhall, Wiltshire
120 St Pancras, Euston Road
121 St Mark's
122 St Giles, Camberwell
123 Church of the Holy Innocents, Higham, Gloucestershire
124 St Cuthbert's, Philbeach Gardens

Acknowledgments

ACKNOWLEDGMENTS

The author and publishers would like to thank the following for their permission to reproduce the photographs used in this book: Gordon Barnes (123); Peter Barnfield (121); F. Frith and Co (30); A. F. Kersting (2, 3, 25, 38, 39, 40, 49, 50, 51, 56, 69, 78, 80, 82, 94, 96, 98, 101, 107, 118, 119, 120, 122); Olive Smith (for photographs by the late Edwin Smith) (99, 124). Nos. 31, 52, 62, 67, 70, 84, 85, 89, 106 are from the publishers' collection.

1
Anglo-Saxon 600-1066

JUST as no subsequent period of architecture begins or ends abruptly at any one point in time, so the origins of Anglo-Saxon work were to be found in the factors which influenced the British under Roman occupation. Then, as afterwards, it was part of a far reaching style of architecture which, local peculiarities notwithstanding, swept northwards from the Mediterranean and into Scandinavia. The comparative geographic isolation of Britain, the distribution and availability of various kinds of building materials and the availability or otherwise of skilled workmen all contributed towards the style of architecture we now call Anglo-Saxon.

The first influence on design was the **basilican plan.** The basilica was a public hall, used throughout the Roman Empire to house law courts and exchanges. It had a rectangular two-celled ground plan; the main body of the hall was usually divided by rows of pillars into two aisles one on each side. Judges or officials sat behind an altar within a circular apse at the west end. A number of the secular buildings in Roman Britain were based on this design. Whilst one can see how readily adaptable it was to church use, it is not clear how or why it came to be chosen, although familiarity may have been an important factor.

All of the earliest churches to be built here whilst Britain belonged to the Roman Empire, and in the southern regions where the influence of Roman Christianity predominated for long afterwards, were in the basilican style. They had similar ground plans to churches abroad but were generally smaller. By the end of the seventh century only the larger and more important buildings were basilican, and these were rarely found outside southern England. Excavations at the Roman town of Silchester, Hampshire, revealed a fourth-century Christian church of this type. It had an aisled nave with western apse, eastern narthex or ante-chamber, and small transepts at the west end of the aisles. Augustine's first cathedral at Canterbury was very similar and had been modelled on St Peter's basilica at Rome.

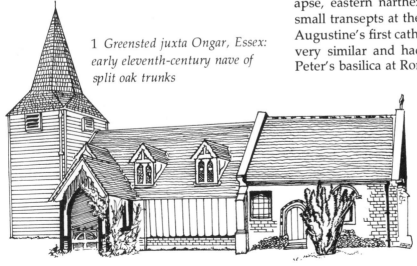

1 *Greensted juxta Ongar, Essex: early eleventh-century nave of split oak trunks*

◄2 *Worth, Sussex: view from the east showing the apsidal chancel*

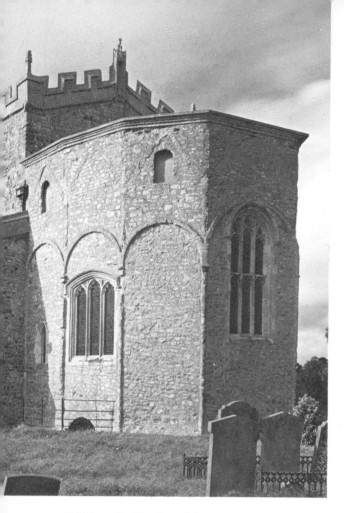

3 *Wing, Buckinghamshire: polygonal Saxon apse*

The apse, which housed a stone altar set on mosaic or coloured tiles to enhance its spiritual importance, was originally semi-circular. Sometimes one was built at either end of the nave, and apses could also be polygonal as at Wing, Buckinghamshire. The cruciform ground plan was formed when transepts were built between – and at right angles to – the nave and apse, forming a crossing in front of it. The two cells were sometimes separated by a single arcade. Augustine's smaller churches, such as Reculver, Kent (demolished 1805) were on the basilican plan but had apses to the east. No one is really sure how or why chancels came to be built to the east of the nave, but certainly the change occurred in Britain very soon after the coming of Augustine.

4 *Bradwell juxta Mare, Essex: an isolated chapel which was once the nave*

The **Celtic plan** originated in Ireland and spread along the same paths as the converting missionaries and saints. These churches were small: a development of the single cells which were the early Celtic sanctuaries, or oratories of the type still to be seen in West Cornwall. The ground plan was a basic two-cell arrangement: a rectangular nave and a smaller rectangular chancel to the east. Generally, these churches were square ended. They were first established in the north and west of England, becoming popular everywhere outside the south and south east, which was dominated by the Roman basilica. In some areas there was fusion of both styles. The simple internal Celtic arrangement and general characteristics were coupled with an apsidal ending. However, although the Anglo Saxons were skilled in building boats and everything from the plentiful supply of timber, they found it difficult to create semi-circular endings in wood, and preferred the square-ended Celtic type. A later example of c.845, the nave wall at Greensted-juxta-Ongar, Essex, shows how they built walls of wood by splitting tree trunks lengthways and setting them up with the flat surface inwards. The tops of the trunks were shaped so that they could be attached by wooden pegs to a plank, and the bases were let into another horizontal piece of wood.

In marked contrast to the arcade of the basilica, there was no structural division between the nave and chancel. If for no other

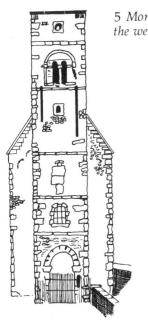

5 *Monkwearmouth, Durham: the west porch and tower*

6 *Escomb, Durham: large blocks of stone in the exterior, eighth century*

buildings were nothing like their successors. They were humble, unpretentious and purely functional.

Their purpose was to keep the elements off the altar, the priests and the people. Would the landowners who built the first wooden churches at their own expense have done so if they could not worship in comparative comfort?

The Saxons were building churches in this country for five centuries and there must have been thousands of them in existence at the Norman Conquest. Most had been built by monks, and we know that masons were brought from Gaul as early as the seventh century. By the tenth century local masons had learnt the principles of construction and

reason, there would rarely have been enough space. For another, the style developed from a small rectangular room into a larger rectangular room, whereas the form of the basilica had long been as it was for a specific purpose by the time it arrived in Britain. Division was not a matter which concerned the Celtic saints, even if it did eventually appeal to the Anglo-Saxon builders.

Even in its infancy, each Anglo-Saxon church possessed its own distinctive features, which is why we now have no two churches which are alike in anything other than ground plan. Certainly they had a number of uniform **characteristics.** Chancels were relatively small in floor area and naves were very high in relation to their width. Today one can go into many churches which are described as, for example, almost wholly fifteenth-century, and find oneself in a nave which is very narrow for its height to the base of the clerestory. Bratton, Wiltshire is a good example. In most such buildings one has good cause to suspect that here was an Anglo-Saxon church of typical proportions and later builders had either worked around the original dimensions or built upon the foundations. Of course Anglo-Saxon

7 *Bradford on Avon, Wiltshire, possibly eighth and tenth centuries*

8 *Wareham, Dorset: seventh century*

9 *Codford St Peter, Wiltshire: ecstatic figure on a ninth-century cross shaft*

10 *Inglesham, Wiltshire: Virgin and child, eleventh century*

were able to do the work themselves. The Anglo-Saxon church was the blueprint for all church building which came after it, and to which every subsequent style conformed.

The best **early Christian art** in this country is to be found on the great stone crosses in the north. Before churches were built Christians continued to worship where they had done in the past, but marked the spot with the symbol of the new faith as influenced by Celtic teaching. They took the idea of vine scroll decoration from the Mediterranean regions and animals and birds from their Germanic origins adopting and adapting them into the beautifully executed vine scroll encompassing minor decorative motifs. This decoration appears elsewhere on fonts and capitals but, generally speaking, the high standard of sculpture was not transferred into the early churches. The themes and motifs were only developed slowly, yet at the time of the Conquest the Anglo-Saxon sculptor was far in advance of his contemporaries across the channel. In fact there had been nothing in northern Europe which, in its original state, could equal the vigour and style of the sculptors in the north of England for the best part of 400 years, although their later crosses were heavier in execution.

Favourite themes of the Anglo Saxons were animals, birds, leaves and vines (the acanthus leaf had made its fleshy appearance by the tenth century) and biblical characters. Our Lord, the Virgin Mary and St John

11 *Bradford on Avon, Wiltshire: angels above the chancel opening*

12 *St Bene'ts, Cambridge: animal carving and impost, tenth century*

13 *Deerhurst, Gloucestershire: animal head, ninth century*

15 *Barnak, Northamptonshire: seated Christ*

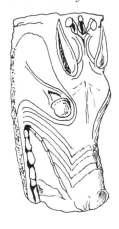

14 *Daglingworth, Gloucestershire: crucifixion, eleventh century*

16 *Breedon-on-the-Hill, Leicestershire: sculpture of the Virgin, ninth century*

17 *Winterbourne Steepleton, Dorset: flying angel, tenth century*

appeared on roods; the Virgin and Child were depicted, as were angels. The sculptors worked with hammer and chisel.

Whilst masons worked in stone, artists of another kind were enriching the church. We know that much was brought from Rome and Gaul in the early days, but in time local craftsmen made wooden carvings, church plate, altar hangings and embroidered altar cloths, vestments, etc. By the tenth century the workshops in English monasteries were turning out bells and carvings, helped by secular labour. Artists and draughtsmen were producing fine paintings and manuscripts and there was some trade in ex-stock church fittings as there was to be in the thirteenth century when there was a vogue for polished marble. Workshops made aumbries to hold the church's ornaments and sacred vessels, and piscinas – the internal drains for the disposal of the water in which the priest washed the vessels or his own hands.

15

The **walls** of Anglo-Saxon stone churches had the appearance of being very solid, even though they were fairly thin. The illusion was helped by their considerable height in relation to the other dimensions and the fact that these large expanses of walls were rarely pierced with lights. And when they were, the openings were very small. The various components which made up the church were rarely set square. There are instances where one side of the nave, chancel, porticus or tower was longer than its opposite wall, and in some cases all four sides of an area were of different lengths. Anglo-Saxon walls were about two and a half feet thick, but a variance of six inches either way was not uncommon.

Walls were made of virtually any materials to hand; rubble and ragstone, clunch and other limestones, flint, chalk, sandstone and re-used Roman bricks. The arches above window openings were sometimes turned with Roman tiles. On top of all this might have been a thin layer of plaster, made out of mixed sand and lime. Some areas had an abundant supply of good natural stone and most of the extant examples of this period are in these areas. Transport was both difficult and costly and it has always been the case that most building stones are better preserved in the areas in which they are quarried or found, and decay quicker if set up in an unfamiliar atmosphere. The Anglo-Saxon mason roughly shaped his stone – if he bothered to do it at all – with an axe, and used the same

tool to dress it. He laid his stones in horizontal courses, and before quoining was introduced turned his angles in an irregular manner. The stones were held together by a mortar which sometimes included crushed Roman bricks. It was very strong. There was usually a sundial on an external wall.

A style of walling which continued from the Roman occupation until well into the Norman period was **herringboning.** This technique consisted of laying horizontal or vertical courses of stones, and placing the stones diagonally in their rows, which alternately inclined to the left and right. It was thought to be a good way of strengthening a wall or giving it support, and for this reason it is more often found in the lower parts. The herringbone method was used in the construction of buildings and field walls as well as to repair them at a later date.

Another feature of Anglo-Saxon walls was the **quoining:** stones placed one on top of the other at the point where two wall surfaces met. Their purpose was to strengthen the structure and they were particularly important where the walls were made of flint or rubble. There were several methods of quoining using flat squared stones, huge irregular blocks or rectangular blocks on end. In early work large stones of varying dimensions were piled one on top of the other, not particularly squarely with their neighbours. Another method involved placing rectangular blocks alternately

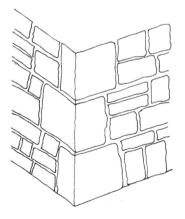

18 *Early walling technique showing megalithic quoins and rough courses*

19 *Jarrow, Durham: section of seventh-century walling*

lengthways and end-on to form the angle. Perhaps the best known term associated with quoining is **long-and-short work,** where lengths of rectangular pillars are set on end separated by shorter lengths with the same area of cross section. It is also used to describe the alternate arrangement of squared, flat stones and large rectangular or square blocks.

Pilaster strips were shallow, rectangular battens which were used to decorate the outside of stone churches in imitation of the struts and beams in the wooden ones. In some cases they were used as structural supports. They are between one foot and three feet deep; four feet to twenty feet in width, and usually climb vertically up the whole wall surface divided only by horizontal string courses. There was long-and-short work in pilasters too. Sometimes short lengths were arranged to make pointed or round arches, 'Y' and 'V' shapes, and used to connect vertical strips. They were a simple, effective way of breaking up flat areas, and were particularly popular from the middle of the tenth century.

Towers of the period were square, rectangular or circular in base area. Although the tallest rarely rise above 70 feet the height is often exaggerated by the relatively small base area; a much wider ratio than in the work of later periods. The first towers were put up in the seventh century, showing how important the church building was considered from early days, that it should physically dominate the domestic and secular architecture around it. They were quite common by the tenth century, being built primarily to house bells but also as places of refuge, lookouts and landmarks. The scarcity of openings in their lower stages and the smallness of any doors may attest to their ulterior role in troubled times and areas.

The Anglo Saxons were not generally so proficient in construction techniques that they could successfully build crossing towers on piers and arches. They were mostly built either over existing one- or two-storey porches which had not originally been designed to take them, or from ground level. There was always an opening through the east wall of the tower into the nave, and at ground level it may have been used as a chapel. Sometimes the priest lived above, with an opening through which he could see into the body of the church.

Some towers were built in a single stage, others in several stages divided by string courses. They either tapered towards the top or had each successive stage narrower than

20 *Earls Barton, Northamptonshire: the tenth-century tower showing pilaster strips*

21 *Barton on Humber, Lincolnshire*

17

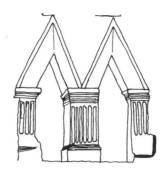

22 *Sompting, Sussex: the eleventh-century tower with 'Rhenish helm' spire*

23 *Deerhurst, Gloucestershire: tower openings*

24 *Monkwearmouth, Durham: tower opening*

the one below. The technique used depended to some extent on the materials available. Internally, each stage probably had a wooden floor and could be climbed by means of ladders. The structure was well equipped – if ill lit – with little windows, arranged in ones and twos on each exposed side of each stage. The belfry stage usually had the most openings, and it is here they are to be found in those Anglo-Saxon towers which are otherwise virtually devoid of windows.

Such towers exist where the whole of the rest of the church fabric is of a later date, because they were probably originally put up against timber naves. Even where this was not the case, many Saxon churches were destroyed between the eleventh and thirteenth centuries – although for a while at least, the original towers were considered adequate. Evidence of the large number of Anglo-Saxon towers which once existed is to be found in the fact that there are now more remains of that period built into our towers than in any other part of the church. There are many instances where the lower stages of tower walls are still of their original material, built before the Conquest.

There has always been more than one connection between towers, porches, transepts and the early porticus. In providing living accommodation for the priest in a structure over the original porch, the precedent was set for a similar upper room to the porch in the later Middle Ages. We know that the ground floor of the tower was often used as a chapel, and that was invariably the purpose of transepts. Their rudimentary forerunner, the porticus, was a kind of large porch against the nave or tower and occasionally the chancel. Whilst its purpose was less certain, some have evidence of an altar and thus of use as a chapel. It may well be that the early transepts were portici, not so placed to make the church cruciform in ground plan but because there was no real distinction between the porch and the transept.

Anglo-Saxon **windows** were small. The masons lacked the knowledge of constructional techniques to produce much else, and there was the overriding problem of the weather. Glass was available but expensive, and either of foreign origin or made by imported labour. It was also thin and easily broken. Benedict Biscop brought glass makers from abroad to teach the craftsmen of this country, but for some unknown reason it was not a skill which the people seemed anxious to attain. More than a century later the Abbot of Wearmouth had to use especially imported Gaulish glassmakers to reglaze his church. In order to let in the maximum light but the minimum bad weather, the early workmen placed their little windows high in the walls and provided them with wooden shutters. Avebury, Wiltshire gives a very good idea of where windows were put in relation to the rest of the Saxon church as shown in the

18

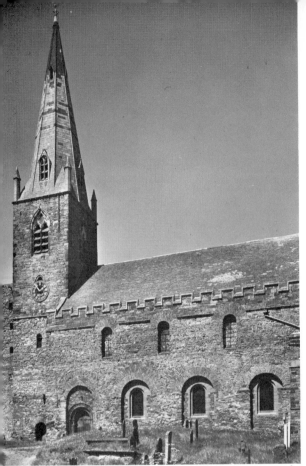

25 *Brixworth church, Northamptonshire, from the south*

body of the church and double windows (or more) in the tower – especially in the upper stages.

Masonry was usually splayed away from the single windows in order to allow more light to come through, and many were cut out of a single, undressed stone. Like the majority of jambs of the period, the sides of these windows frequently inclined towards the top, giving the opening a wider base. The earliest opening of this type was placed more or less flush with the outside wall. It had a single internal splay which, as well as giving a much larger interior opening, might be virtually twice the area of the actual window. One which was placed centrally in the wall and double splayed (i.e. outwards and inwards) is an example of late pre-Conquest work, or was otherwise done in the years immediately following.

The sides of Anglo-Saxon windows were rarely moulded, although – especially in the case of double openings – the feature was often surrounded by a thin moulding of rib work which projected slightly from the surface of the wall. Decoration in double (or more) lights was confined to that on the **balusters.** Belfry openings were made by cutting round-headed, straight-sided holes through the wall and dividing the result with one or more balusters or shafts. These fat pillars were in idea the forerunners of the slender Gothic mullions, even if they did not themselves actually develop these forms. They resembled wood turned on a lathe and were undoubtably copied by the early masons from the work they had been used to doing in wood. They bulged at the centre or were less commonly straight sided, and were usually set up between flat, squared stones. One formed the impost between the arch on either side, and the other was the base. Both the impost – and in some cases a capital – and the base were sometimes corbelled away from the wall surface or otherwise seem to be suspended upon it. One can see the gradual development of this feature throughout the Anglo-Saxon period, from a single plain shaft

dimensions of the present nave. They also used oiled linen, parchment and skins to keep out the elements, but, like closed shutters, these also kept out the light. Anglo-Saxon churches would have been very dark at the best of times.

Most windows of this period were straight sided and round headed. Some had triangular heads and others were wholly circular. It has been suggested that those of the latter type which were placed in a row at clerestory height at Avebury might have been from an even earlier wattle-and-daub church. They are pierced through single pieces of stone with a series of small holes around the centre light. These once held rods to act as a splay through the walling. The arrangement here and elsewhere shows the symmetry and logical order with which masons could approach their overall design. They also had a fairly rigid pattern: single windows as a rule in the

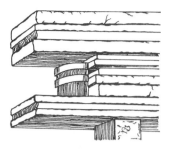

26 *Barnak, Northamptonshire: impost*

27 *Netheravon, Wiltshire: Saxo-Norman capital*

to one between elaborately carved or moulded capitals or bases made out of separate stones. The most common decoration of the baluster was a number of raised or carved out bands, sculpted at various intervals along its length. This feature is to be met several centuries later in the woodwork of Jacobean and Elizabethan times, of which it was something of a hallmark.

The first doorways were portals through the west wall of the cell, or of the tower where one existed, and the ground floor was used as a chapel. They were small but tall in relation to their width; mainly round headed or triangular. In time the single western portal gave way to doorways in the north and south walls near the west end of the nave, occasionally opening into porticus or side chapels. Less frequently they appeared at the east end of the nave in the more familiar position of transepts, and sometimes centrally. They are usually plain and unmoulded, occasionally with a square lintel; but mostly the arches rest on large blocks of stone for imposts. These may be plain, decorated, moulded, or have a chamfered (cut away) under edge. Some are formed by a

28 *Escomb, Durham: doorway*

29 *Somerford Keynes, Gloucestershire: doorway*

number of flat, projecting stones above those of the jambs. Although many jambs were made with large blocks of stone, and some included baluster shafts, the Anglo-Saxon masons seemed unsure of the ability of their structure to carry the weight from above. They compensated by reducing the distance between the jambs towards the top. The doorway was generally left undecorated, although in some instances a shallow hood moulding of flat rib work was placed right around it on the wall surface to ground level.

Much of the above also applies to Anglo-Saxon **arches**, which were round headed and sometimes faced or turned with Roman bricks. As with doorways, they were often cut straight through the wall. Imposts were not always used but occasional wall mouldings broke the stark line of thick stone shafts.

Crypts were cells or chapels built underneath the body of the church, usually at the east end beneath the high altar. They had their origins in the *confessio* of the Roman basilica, and the underground room was kept when this building was taken as the model for the Christian church in this country. Even so, crypts were rare in Anglo-Saxon churches, and were mostly to be found in the buildings which were put up by the well travelled missionaries. Before local craftsmen had the knowledge to beautify their own churches – and even when they could – monks and missionaries accumulated large amounts of religious art and treasures from their visits abroad, particularly to the Mediterranean regions. The crypt was a convenient place to store, exhibit and perhaps hide the treasures and sacred relics which had been collected by pilgrims abroad.

The walls were thick, the ceilings were vaulted in stone and some crypts were divided into a central area and a surrounding walkway – known as an ambulatory – by an arcade. This allowed freedom of movement for those who came to visit. Those at Hexham and Ripon are of this type. The interior of the crypt could be viewed by a hagioscope in the

nave, and it was usually approached down a spiral staircase from either the nave or a transept. A particularly fine example is at Repton, Derbyshire.

Piers were usually square or cylindrical, but short. Bases were made of roughly cut square blocks of stone left quite plain, as were abaci. This is not to say that the Anglo Saxons did not occasionally show some inventive flair. The crypt at Repton has four quite slender pillars which taper and are decorated with spiral bands.

Infants were first baptised in **fonts** in the second century AD. The practice had become general by the sixth century, and was compulsory in England from 816. To begin with the font was positioned near the west end of the building in the centre of the nave, because the service of Baptism began either in

30 *Bradford on Avon, Wiltshire: doorway from the north porticus into the nave*

31 *Repton, Derbyshire: the Saxon crypt*

32 *Potterne, Wiltshire: tub-shaped font bowl*

Very few fonts now ascribed to this period in England are known to have been embellished with other than a simple inscription or a plain or cable moulding. Such decoration as there was may even have been copied from the Roman remains which were still about. It has always been extremely difficult to date Saxon fonts accurately, especially those which are of plain, unmoulded stone. Few can be recognised by the infrequent and crude carvings. Avebury, Wiltshire, has a tub which has been assigned to this period, as has the bucket-shaped bowl at Potterne in the same county. Deerhurst, Gloucestershire, has the best preserved of its type. Its date was deduced as the ninth century on the evidence of the Celtic trumpet spiral decoration with which it is carved, bordered by a vine scroll motif of Northumbrian influence. It rests on a pillar which is thought to be part of what was once a Saxon cross. A light interlacing of Celtic origin similarly dates the bowl at Washaway, Cornwall, and nearby Morwenstow has such a misshapen oddity that it must surely be Saxon.

the western porch or doorway if no porch existed. None of the original wooden fonts have survived and the remaining examples of Saxon fonts which are made of stone are all roughly circular and of tub shape. They follow the design of the wooden barrels, themselves a continental innovation.

Not all pre-Conquest items now described as fonts were such in their early days, nor are they all of the tub shape. An Anglo-Saxon cross or shaft socket with ornamentation of Roman influence would have made a square font for later people, or might have been used in part to support a later bowl. The fonts at Melbury Bubb in Dorset and Wilne, Derbyshire have both been carved out of the circular section from pre-Conquest cross shafts and set upside down. At Dolton, Devonshire two blocks from a Saxon cross stand one on top of the other; a squared block supporting a tapering 'bowl'.

2
Norman 1066-1160 and Transitional 1150-1200

THE Anglo Saxons developed a style of Romanesque which, even with its own local and regional characteristics, was not dissimilar to the architecture in Normandy where Edward the Confessor (r. 1041–66) spent his youth. The abbey which he began at Westminster c. 1050, was a showpiece for the most advanced schools of the day. Parts of it now represent the earliest Norman work in England, originally heralding what was soon to come – at first in relatively small measure. The Normans' immediate pre-occupation with large ecclesiastical buildings such as abbeys and cathedrals, and the necessity for castles, meant that the humble parish church remained almost entirely Anglo-Saxon in concept and execution until about 1080. Edward's reign saw little activity in either church building or ecclesiastical matters. In 1062 Stigand was appointed Archbishop of Canterbury over a slothful and corrupt church. He was to be favoured by the Conqueror although excommunicated by a succession of Popes and finally imprisoned. He was replaced by Lanfranc in 1070.

William I introduced a great revival in religious matters, re-establishing Roman precedents and thereby conforming the country to European Christianity. The aged Lanfranc proved to be a tireless worker, reforming and rebuilding the monasteries and initiating a new era in church building. The Council of London, 1075, moved bishoprics to large centres and cathedrals were started in the Norman style at Canterbury, Lincoln, London St Pauls, Rochester, St Albans,

Winchester and Worcester. This trend was halted by William II (r. 1087–1100) who made great demands on the church. He took bishoprics and abbeys either for himself or to rent, ensuring a tough time for Anselm who had succeeded Lanfranc at Canterbury in 1093.

Henry I came to the throne in 1100 at a time when attention had shifted from the large foundations to the small parish churches. Most of them were timber structures which had been put up before the Conquest and were to be swept away in a massive programme of rebuilding which occupied the first half of the twelfth century. Henry created bishoprics at Carlisle and Ely, established an abbey at Reading and restored many of the old ones which had fallen into neglect. By the time Stephen became king in 1135 the church's power was so immense that it was little curtailed in the period of anarchy and civil strife which followed. More than 150 further monasteries were established, and a great age of parish church building ended at about the same time as Stephen's reign in 1154. Between then and 1189 when Henry II's reign ended the church enjoyed massive support, due largely to the King's quarrel with Becket, and the Norman style of church building gradually gave way to the Gothic.

Although the task could not have been altogether in their hearts, it was the English who were set to work on the new churches and built them very much in what had become their native style. The Norman style was not fully developed either here or across the

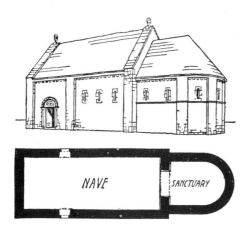

33 *Plan of the original twelfth-century apsidal building (scale 36 feet to one inch)*

34 *Hales, Norfolk: Saxo-Norman church*

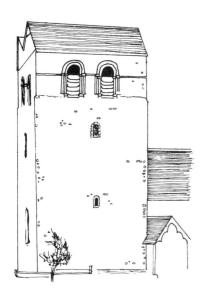

36 *Tixover, Leicestershire: solid three-stage tower*

35 *Fingest, Buckinghamshire: massive tower with double saddleback roof*

37 *Barfreston, Kent*

channel until the twelfth century, and at all times Anglo-Saxon church art and sculpture was far in advance of it. The first Norman churches to be built in England after the Conquest were solid-looking and solemn, virtually devoid of any sculptural decoration or colour. But even if they lacked freedom of expression in an artistic sense, the smallest of them must have seemed grand in scale to the English, though functional in the manner of castles and fortifications.

Norman architectural design developed at the same rate in England during the last 30 years of the eleventh century as it did in Normandy, but church building rushed ahead. The idea was to furnish every village with a place of worship and, as a result, almost every mediaeval church which still remains is Norman in origin.

Although the Conquerors brought with them a revival of the apse, the most common ending to churches in their own country, it was almost wholly confined to the south-eastern counties. Here had been the stronghold of that feature in the past, and they were now better in touch with the origins of the new regime. The three-celled plan – nave, choir and sanctuary – prevailed. In the two-celled plan, the width and height of each section were often equal. When a tower was added it was most usually axial above the choir in the case of a square east end, and to the west of the nave where the east end was apsidal. The high altar was placed to allow a processional way or retro-choir behind it. The Normans continued to build two- or three-celled churches of this type until more space was needed to accommodate the ever increasing number of worshippers. Until that time the smaller two-celled church tended to have a nave/chancel length ratio of 2:1. Transepts were added north and south of the choir, forming the first real cruciform churches, and the towers above became crossing towers. Small apsidal chapels were sometimes built out of the east walls of the transepts.

The aisleless nave was most common for a new church building before the thirteenth century, despite the fact that the Normans were finding it necessary to extend and develop not only the churches which had come before them but also their own. Rarely did they add one aisle to the nave without at least planning another, but equally rarely were they built simultaneously. The north aisle usually came first because there were few burials on that side of the church, to be followed by an aisle to the south. Most naves – particularly those on Anglo-Saxon foundations – were narrow; aisles were usually built of equal width and rarely more than half that of the nave. The problem of taking the nave further away from the source of natural light resulted in the clerestory. It was formed by raising the walls of the nave above the new arcades and opening them out into lights. The space between the top of an arcade and the clerestory is called a triforium.

The layman probably recognises Norman work more by its profusion of **surface decoration** than anything else. **Chevron or zig zag,** the characteristic 'V'-shape moulding of the period, made its first appearance early in the twelfth century and soon became the most widely used surface decoration for arches of all kinds. It was followed by smaller motifs, either abutting or repeated at regular intervals, mostly arranged in single or double rows.

Billet consisted of short raised rectangles with either a square or semi-circular cross section like small lengths of fillet or roll moulding. It was sometimes put up in alternating triple rows, when it is known as **alternate billet. Indented** moulding was basically the flat 'V' shape of chevron, carved out so that its background was the same shape, reversed. One of the most common was **bead** or its larger form of **pellet.** These were plain spheres of different sizes which could be used as a feature in themselves or as secondary decoration almost everywhere. **Lozenge** was a diamond, usually wider horizontally than vertically. This was also true of **double cone;** a diamond shape rounded,

38 *Kilpeck, Herefordshire, from the east*

conoid at the leading edge and blunt at the point of contact with its neighbour. **Nail-head** was a four-sided, raised pyramid set square and done in continuous sequence. **Star** ornament was similar in conception but was cut away on each side to form a figure with a point at each angle. The raised outline of battlements was depicted on **embattled** moulding, a name also applied to raised triangular shapes which have chamfered leading edges. Much twelfth century work is bound by a **cable** moulding. This took the form of a twisted cord and came in a whole range of thicknesses. It sometimes looked like loosely intertwined string but was more usually done as a thick roll, occasionally quite out of proportion to the feature it adorned. The decorative moulding which contained more ornamentation than any other was **medallion**, the oval shape which was frequently formed with a tiny bead and included little carvings within and between each piece.

The **beak head,** a favourite form of

39 *Stewkley, Buckinghamshire, from the north west*

decoration, takes us more into that field of sculpture which includes the ornamentation on corbel tables. The heads of birds, animals, dragons and grotesques were given a long beak or pointed chin which extended over a convex moulding to the roll below. Sometimes a whole row was painstakingly done almost identically, but rows of beakheads may otherwise include several different forms. In their misshapen state they are meant to represent the servants of the devil, ready to capture the souls of those who come lightly to church.

When the sculptors carved beasts and grotesques elsewhere they were producing tangible representations of the fears in their own minds, of the half beliefs which lingered on from pagan times, or a derivation of the art culled from many sources. They carved birds, fishes and animals – which in many cases they could never have seen – because they were symbolic or of some Christian significance. They sculpted the people around them, likenesses of important people of whom they had heard, and the everyday things in their lives such as shells, flowers and foliage, fir cones and the tools of their trades.

The **walls** of Norman churches have the appearance of being thick and solid. In fact they had a core of rubble infilling between skins of dressed stones which were more or less square on the exposed surfaces. The masons worked diagonally with an axe, producing deep, uneven strokes on the faced ashlar or cut stones. This was bonded together by coarse mortar, and a large amount was needed in the wide joints of early Norman work. The blocks were better abutted as the period progressed. Even so, the general thickness of the walls was necessary because they were not otherwise supported; an omission which was to give structural problems when the time came to widen arches and impose other loads on them.

The period saw the introduction of **buttresses** in the sense that projections were built from ground level against the exterior wall, in contrast to the Saxon pilasters which appeared at many points on the wall surface. Although these were much wider, they projected but a few inches, were of equal depth along their length and thereby of little use as supports. Rectangular in surface area, Norman buttresses were usually quite plain, built in one stage with their upper surfaces sloping towards the cornice or eaves of the roof. Like pilasters, they were really there to break up the stark surface of the walls and to mark the extent of bays. Some later examples had thin shafts let into the outer angles. A projection of this kind which extends an equal distance along both walls from the angle at which they meet is known as a clasping buttress or pilaster, and first made its appearance in the twelfth century.

The wall surface continued to be broken up horizontally by **string courses,** first with a square cross section but chamfered along the lower surface angle. They had a heavy outline, and were often enriched by small

decorative motifs of the period. The most common (and later) variation had both angles chamfered with a quarter round between, along the leading edge. In some cases a chamfered upper edge developed into a fillet, thence to a roll on the underside. Other string courses of the period were basically square in cross section with varying combinations of slight hollows and rolls. They ran right around the building, inside and out, tying it together and giving a feeling of security. The usual level of the string course was below that of the window sill, although they occasionally

40 *St Nicholas, New Romney, Kent: the tower*

ran over the head of a window arch forming hood mouldings or dripstones. For the most part, however, they died into the wall whenever they came across intervening obstacles such as doorways or buttresses.

In many cases the string courses were made the basis of the rich surface ornamentation which was to come later, particularly the profusion of fine **arcading** which became a feature of towers, belfries and west fronts externally, and the interior walls of chancels. The masons went in for blind (unpierced) surface arcading around openings such as windows and small doorways, to which it was often similar in design and dimensions. Sometimes the feature was simply included in the overall design of the piece, but in all cases served to enhance it. Where such decoration was put up on only one interior wall, this was generally to the north. Even the simplest blind arcade gave the wall a rich appearance; more so when it was decorated with the typical mouldings of the period, and at its best when the heads were intersected and decorated.

The other external decorative feature applied to walls was the **corbel table,** a Norman innovation. A corbel is a small block of stone which helps to support a roof, parapet or cornice. Sometimes it is at the end of a shaft. A row of them, usually connected, makes a corbel table and such are to be found both inside and outside churches which date from the eleventh century. Some of the blocks were plain, but more often they were carved with either human, animal and grotesque heads or decorative motifs of the time.

The plentiful supply of timber meant that this was the cheapest material for the trussed rafters of the steep pitched **roofs,** and the tie beams across the nave and chancel. It was also the most workable material for the technology of the times. The tie beams were set close together and used as battens for the flat boarding of the ceiling. The heavy tie beam completed the triangle with the equally rude rafters (see figure 97 page 76). Until this time roofs had been held up by angled timbers joined to each other at the apex, and repeated at

41 *Iffley, Oxfordshire: the lavishly decorated west front*

42 *St John's Devizes, Wiltshire. The crossing tower dominates Norman and Perpendicular work at the east end*

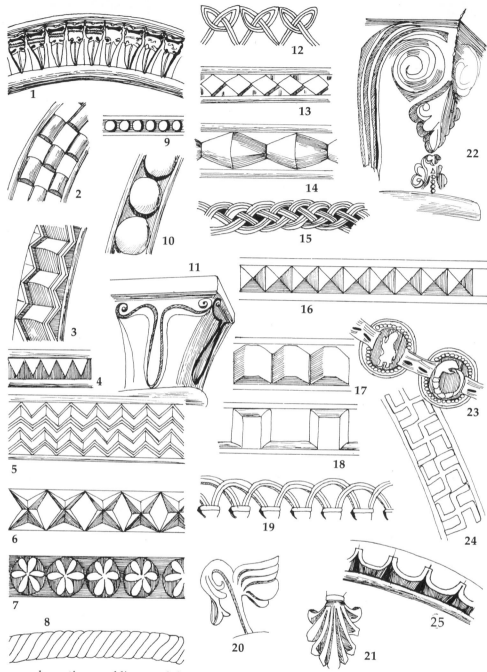

43 *Norman decorative mouldings and decoration*

1 Beakhead	**10** Pellet	**17, 18** Embattled
2 Alternate billet	**11** Waterleaf	**19** Interlacing
3, 4 and **5** Chevron or zig zag types	**12** Knotwork	**20, 21** Leaf forms
6 Star	**13** Lozenge	**22** Volute and leaf forms
7 Six-lobed flower	**14** Double cone	**23** Medallion
8 Cable	**15** Plait	**24** Key
9 Bead	**16** Nail-head	**25** Scallop

frequent intervals. Stability was given to the structure by inserting a horizontal beam which connected pairs of rafters at some point along their length. The Normans knew how to construct a simple barrel vault in stone, but did not have enough confidence in the ability of their walls to take the weight. Early stone vaulting was confined to small areas where the perimeter walls were low, such as porches and crypts. It was done over the chancel and the narrow aisles, but never across the nave which was always roofed with wood.

The masons learnt to produce a groined vault by intersecting two barrel vaults at right angles, and to add ribs which were later moulded and had bosses at the intersections. By the end of the period quadripartite and sexpartite vaults were appearing. The former was one which had four sections of equal size, divided by transverse diagonal ribs which crossed in the centre. The latter was similarly sectioned but included an additional rib which divided the vault into six unequal parts.

Towers no longer provided the main entrance to the church, and became no more than supports for belfries. Only those still in use as nave towers played a part in church services. It was a period of peace and stability so they had no use as lookout or refuge. Yet they continued to give importance to the building, allowing it physically to dominate its surroundings.

In many cases the Normans built upon Anglo-Saxon west porches, thickening the walls where necessary. But they had also developed the technique of supporting a central tower with piers placed only at the angles, and this proved to be the most important advance in the design of towers. It enabled crossing towers to become a standard feature, bringing the tower physically into the body of the church from out of which it seemed to rise as the crowning glory. It also enabled the underside, walls and features to be richly treated with the decoration of the day, embodying it in the general fabric. Towers were mostly built with a square or rectangular base plan, but were circular where there was a lack of good building stone. They were low and massive. Where transepts already existed the base area was determined by the widths of the nave and transepts and was therefore more usually wider from north to south.

Although wooden spires with up to six sides were not unknown, most Norman towers had low, pyramidal caps covered in stone or – more commonly – wooden roofing tiles. Few had parapets. Some had saddleback or double saddleback roofs, a popular style in northern Europe. In this the two opposite walls of the tower were gabled and the apex was formed by a roof ridge. The responsibility for the exterior **stair turret** also rests with this period. It is an unnecessary adjunct which interrupts the visual line of the tower. It was built from the ground to just below the belfry stage where the top was usually angled into the wall. Stair turrets were either circular or octagonal in area.

Windows were set high up and flush with the exterior wall surface, but deeply splayed on the inside for maximum natural light. The openings were small and narrow and for the most part single lights, although groups of three were sometimes placed in the east wall of the chancel above the altar. Few remain because the subsequent need to let more natural light into the building meant that they were too small. This was true even in larger churches where the openings were bigger. They had to be replaced. In view of the way in

44 *Highworth, Wiltshire: carving, probably tympanum*

which later builders tried to retain Norman decorative work one can imagine these windows being removed with some regret, for they came to be as beautifully adorned as the other arched features of the period.

The openings had round heads and straight sides, set in arches made of small irregular blocks of cut stones with mortar between. When the vogue for arch ordering was at its height the window was often recessed and treated in a way similar to the doorways and chancel arches which were being put up with a riot of decorative carving. The inner arch of the window was often moulded with the characteristic zig zag or other kind of linked decoration such as diamond or bead. Such decoration might be continued around the head and right down to the sill. Little decorative shafts with caps and bases were put up and there were two or three orders of recessed arches. The exposed surfaces around windows were magnificently carved or incised with the ornamentation of the day and, if the window had a hood moulding, that too often included a diaper pattern.

This period also introduced the circular window into clerestories and towers, a design which looked particularly effective when used in conjunction with zig zag moulding. From it developed the wheel window, product of breaking up the circular light by inserting radiating shafts. In early work these shafts

had caps and bases; a clumsy start to what was to develop into the beautiful rose window of High Gothic. Norman clerestory windows were generally larger than those of the nave.

Very few **porches** were built before the thirteenth century; a strange fact in view of the time and workmanship which had been put into doorways over the preceding 200 years. Those which were erected tended to be shallow, although some of the larger ones had an upper room or parvise. Since the area to roof was small, it was sometimes barrel vaulted.

Doorways competed with chancel arches as the most striking single feature in churches of the eleventh and twelfth centuries, and were at their richest from c. 1130. Most were protected from the elements before it was too late to stop them from being irreparably eroded, and they remained in such good condition that they were retained by the restoring Victorians. By the middle of the eleventh century the main doorway was no longer on the west side, but in the south wall of the nave. As the point of entry for everyone and the beginning of so many acts of worship, it was of unparalleled importance and the sculptors tried to enrich it accordingly.

45 *Old Shoreham, Sussex: the crossing tower*

46 *Colney St Andrew, Norfolk: round, single stage tower with double-splayed lights*

To begin with the doorway was plain, round-headed and straight-sided. A recessed tympanum continued to be a feature between the arch and the square lintel below. It was sometimes an arrangement of stone blocks, perhaps of two colours, forming a pattern. Fairly plain symbols were carved on a flat background, or an overall diaper pattern was carved featuring small decorative motifs or shapes of the period. In time whole scenes came to be carved above the doorway, many loosely connected in some way with the theme of the triumph of good over evil. The tree of life was a favourite, and foliage, vines, animals and fishes abounded – most of which had some liturgical significance. It was a popular spot to carve Christ in Majesty with suitable attendants, the Harrowing of Hell, and the grotesques which personified the fears of the sculptors.

The doorway beneath had bold roll mouldings which were often carved into a thick cable with shallow decoration such as a flat bead, star ornament or diaper pattern between the roll or on the hood. The arch was supported on either side by a circular shaft with a cushion cap and square base. Each recessed arch in a receding group is known as an order, and in the course of the period Norman doorways, as also chancel arches, came to be made up of several orders. Where the mouldings were not continued all around the arch to ground level, each order was supported by recessed piers engaged in the jambs. To these and the arches above were accorded the lavish and detailed ornamentation of the day: a wild profusion of decorative motifs. Animal heads, grotesques or foliage were favoured as the stops on hood mouldings.

There was often a north door to the nave, known as the 'Devil's door'. It was left open during the service of Baptism in the belief that any evil spirits in the child would escape through it. Although such doors might later be protected by substantial porches, they were rarely treated in such a lavish fashion as their southern counterpart.

Doors were made out of vertical planks of oak, horizontally battened on the inside and

47 *Roughton St Mary, Norfolk*

48 *St Michael, Oxford: late with twin bell openings*

strengthened on the outside by bands of iron. Where there were three of these, the centre one was usually plain, whereas the others were decoratively shaped.

The semi-circular **arch** was the main type to be built in Norman churches before the middle of the twelfth century. The stilted arch, where the perpendicular jambs continued briefly above the impost, was not unknown but was rare, as was the slightly bulging horseshoe shape. The huge blocks of stone which had formed the width of the jambs in a single length gave way to the smaller pieces of cut stone on the surface with an infilling of rubble. Arches were higher and wider, but of a shape not designed to withstand great weights from above or sideways thrusts; besides which, the height of a round arch cannot be more than half its distance across. This is why many chancel arches have now dropped, and their piers incline outwards at the imposts. Indeed the same is often true of whole nave arcades, which now seem to lean perilously out of true. That so many have survived is not so much a testimony to the skill of the builder as to the fact that they were low and had relatively little weight to support.

The chancel arch was lavishly sculptured, but usually only on its west face. Arches were often of several orders, and similarly treated. The zig zag was very deeply cut, either along the surface of the wall or at right angles to it. Blind arcading was sometimes used in juxtaposition to a chancel arch; one set either side helped to enhance the feature.

A **pier** is the whole structure between the floor of the church and the point above from which an arch springs. During this period it attained its most complete form, comprising abacus, capital, shaft, base and plinth. It became more decorative in both shape and applied ornamentation than the basic structural necessity it had been.

In early Norman work the abacus was plain and square, derived from the shape of its block capital forerunner. The under edge was either chamfered or rounded off, then plainly moulded. Later all surfaces of the abacus were treated with the small mouldings and decorative motifs of the period. The capital beneath began as a variation on the cushion shape, the early Norman form consisting of a square upper section which had its lower angles rounded off into an ornamental convex shape towards the pillar below. This developed with fluted, scalloped and trumpet scalloped underside. Leaves and beads appeared between the scallops, and the latter often linked other decorative features. Gradually the mass of Norman decoration spread all over the capital, often broken up by leaf forms at the angles. The volute – the spiral twist copied from designs on Ionic capitals – made its appearance at the corners, often covering the whole depth of the capital. Much of this work would have been painted.

The capital was usually separated from the shaft by a narrow roll moulding or fillet. As a general rule the bigger the Norman shaft or pillar the earlier it is likely to be of its type. Most of those put up in country churches were cylindrical; some were octagonal and these were occasionally alternated with cylindrical ones in the same arcade. Some of the taller cylindrical piers had horizontal bands of ornamentation in the centre; others were frequently adorned with carved network, spiral decoration, zig zag or cable moulding. Square pillars were also common, and some of them were massive; later examples of these had slender shafts at each of the angles. In the course of time virtually all the ornamentation which the sculptors of this period applied to their arcades found its way in miniature to the pillars. The shafts associated with lavishly decorated chancel arches were sometimes hardly recognisable as such for the profusion of carvings on them.

The Norman base was usually a bold roll moulding, plain ovolo with the occasional flat fillet above. In cross section the mouldings were round or quarter round with shallow hollows between. The **plinth** was either circular or square and was made out of a plain, unmoulded block of stone. It sometimes had a tongue, spur or piece of decorative foliage

50 *St John's, Devizes, Wiltshire: the Norman chancel*

51 *Tickencote, Rutland: the chancel arch*

curving outwards towards each of the four corners.

The **piscina** had been little more than a hole in the floor since Pope Leo IV decreed such an outlet for holy water in the ninth century. The Normans had a wall model – a drain within a basin, protruding from a low niche – but favoured the **pillar piscina.** This was a small bowl on top of a low shaft. The water which the priest used to wash his own hands or the sacred vessels drained down a vertical bore through the shaft. As they were always set up by an altar, many early piscinas remain as a guide to the former position of altars which have since disappeared. In the chancel, the piscina was often incorporated into the design of **sedilia,** the set of up to four recessed seats which were used by the priest and his assistants. Those of the Norman period were built beneath characteristic round arches.

Early Norman **fonts** were plain, unmounted stone tubs. They developed into cubical and cylindrical bowls, mounted on pedestals. The main designs used by the Normans for their fonts were circular unmounted, circular mounted on a central stem, circular mounted on a central stem with several other supports – either as a decoration or in a functional capacity, square unmounted – usually on thick corner colonnettes and sometimes with a central stem, cup and chalice shaped mounted and unmounted, and octagonal. Most of the unmounted cylindrical fonts which have survived are from the first few years after the Conquest. In the twelfth century a font bowl was most commonly made from a single block of stone, hewn to shape inside and out.

Never again was carving to be so enthusiastically done with quite so much gay abandon, rustic figurework and irreverent mixture of the sacred and profane. The Normans carved what they loved the most and what they feared the greatest: themselves and many forms of the unknown. Permanent materials were used. An innovation of the period was the use of

52 *Melbourne, Derbyshire: massive piers of the nave arcade*

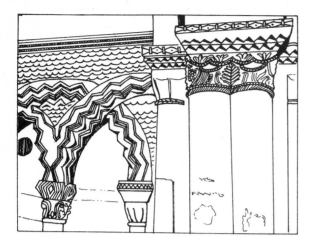

53 *Devizes, Wiltshire: Norman enrichment*

54 *Stapleford, Wiltshire: the nave arcade*

55 *Stanton Fitzwarren, Wiltshire: font*

lead as a construction material, although it was often used as a lining except with impervious stones such as purbeck marble or granite.

The period was to develop almost infinite variety of decoration, beginning with a small amount of crude carving. Designs reflected in relief the cushion capitals and shafts of the period, and from the eleventh century arcading became the standard design on font bowls. Much to be found elsewhere in the church was depicted in miniature. The majority of bowls had a moulding at some point around their circumference, most commonly near the top or at the foot where they are known as base mouldings. String courses were either of interlaced or plaited cables of varying thicknesses and widths or single, plain rolls which tended to be thinner than the cables.

The most common base moulding was either two heavy, plain rolls set one on top of the other or with a hollow between. Most bowls were supported by a cylindrical pillar, plain except, occasionally, for an annulet. Several supporting shafts were not always of the same thickness. The Norman plinth was usually thick, and could be square, round or octagonal. The twelfth century also produced the spur. This was a raised claw-like protrusion from the font's base moulding to its plinth,

and was popular for about 100 years.

A number of regional styles were evolved. The Aylesbury district of Buckinghamshire has eight, richly decorated, hemispherical bowls. Each is reminiscent of an inverted capital of the period. Their similar basic features include an upper band of decoration, a fluted underside separated by some form of moulding from a (in most cases) square base. These take the form of inverted, scalloped cushion capitals with decoration on the double or single lunettes of each side. Elsewhere the decoration differs. The Hereford group has single, double and triple string plaiting together with knot shapes as well as loose weave, fine figure and animal sculpture. The Bodmin type is of a short, central stem supporting a cup shaped bowl with four merely decorative legs at the corners. The Launceston group has a distinct cushion-capital shape supported by a single shaft, with carved heads at the corners of the bowls and, in many cases, the space between is filled by a six-lobed flower within a circle, the whole ringed by a serpent or snake with a head at each end. The Feock group comprise circular bowls which include diagonal crosses, circles, rosettes, zig zag and the common tree of life theme. North Norfolk has a group of heavy square bowls which stand on colonnettes and are very intricately carved. The Sussex type has a plain square bowl, tapering downwards, on a central stem and four corner supports.

Several large, square Norman bowls were made from dark Tournai marble, imported from Belgium. They are either supported by a central shaft, or four pillars at the angles. The bowls have fine figure sculpture depicting Biblical scenes, or are otherwise adorned with grotesques.

56 St Nicholas, Brighton: font

Transitional 1150–1200

For a while the old monastic orders vied with the new and with the builders and masons who were seeking new ways of expressing their developing skills. The Benedictines, who had come with St Augustine, and other orders which followed them, conservatively clung to the Romanesque as did – generally speaking – the south and east of the country. The austere Cistercians arrived in 1128 and spread westward, along the border with Wales and into Yorkshire. By design there was no place in their buildings for the decorative riot to be found elsewhere, and it was from the areas under their influence that the early Gothic emerged.

As builders, masons and sculptors refined their arts, the work was wrought with a greater delicacy of feeling. The hammer and chisel replaced the axe and gave better results. Religious feeling was strong; there were around 500 monastic establishments in the country in the middle of the twelfth century. The vertical development in church architecture might have been as much the result of man's psychological desire to reach God as it was of his improved skills. At the least, one complemented and encouraged the other.

The source of the pointed arch in England, the earliest important break with the Romanesque, has never firmly been established. In a way, it had been around for most of the twelfth century. It was the resulting shape between the left-hand column supporting a round-headed arch in an interlaced arcade, and the right-hand column beneath the arch before it. But this was a purely decorative feature whereas the first Transitional pointed arches were constructional.

It has been suggested that the influence for the pointed arch might have been the architecture of the east, noticed by western knights involved in the Crusades. Certainly it first appears in England c. 1160 just after the failure of the Second Crusade, but some 37

57 *Climping, Sussex: transitional Norman tower on an Early English church*

years before Richard I became involved in the Crusades. By then the pointed arch was commonplace, giving credence to the third and more generally accepted possibility: that it arose through problems encountered in vaulting a rectangular area to the same height without using stilted arches on the shorter sides. It came down from the vaulting when builders realised that it made possible much taller buildings.

For a while the round-headed arch and the new pointed ones were put up side by side, in such a way that one can see in how short a space of time the latter took effect. The two might be put up in juxtaposition at a tower crossing; a round chancel arch appeared next to a pointed nave arcade – both done within a very few years of each other. Round arches appeared with deep, hollow mouldings. The use of the chisel enabled orders to be chamfered, producing a less sharp effect. Pointed arches were put up with heavy roll mouldings and typical Norman decoration, zig-zag, etc., but more sharply cut. Above them is often the contrast of a clerestory of small, round-headed lights.

Round arches were raised above capitals which had the beginnings of stiff leaf on them, although nicely done scalloped capitals continued to be popular. A squashy **waterleaf** made its appearance; this was the leaf shape which began in the centre of each face of the capital, curling upwards and outwards towards the abacus, but finally ending on an inward curve. The sectional **plantain leaf** was developed during the Transitional period. Flat and broad, it was eminently suitable for decorating fonts.

The pillar below took on a more slender form, round and octagonal pillars sometimes alternating in the same arcade.

The heights of towers increased, and round belfry openings were sometimes contained within pointed arches. Walls were thinner, although still thick. Masonry was more finely jointed and the stones were better worked. Single-light windows were made larger, there were more of them and they were given deeper splays. New pointed ones were occasionally put up with typical Norman decoration. As the masons became more skilful this was carved in increasingly bolder relief, being more deeply cut. Purbeck marble made its appearance as shafts – firstly as clusters during this period of transition – and became a popular material for font bowls.

3
Early English 1200-1300

THE period of architecture which the Victorians liked the least, but to which they accorded the descriptive term 'First Pointed', was peculiar to England in the years between Romanesque and geometrical Gothic. It was a time when genuine religious feeling finally overcame barbaric enthusiasm in church architecture and art. Simplicity and purity were the basic criteria, done in a way which emphasised features through the play of light and shade. The development of the previous 40 years inspired a subtler spirit which made itself felt in a more delicate line and contour, and in essence rather than bulk.

Richard was obsessed with the Crusades, and his absence from his kingdom during almost the whole of his reign (1189–99) helped the church to increase its power, and its influence over the people. Monastic orders continued to be established and to reform the church. Although John (r. 1199–1216) plundered the church and opposed the appointment of Stephen Langton to Canterbury, the Archbishop successfully led the barons along the road to Magna Carta. In so doing he acquired the following of an influential sector of the people, and became the first of a succession of great churchmen who were to make their marks on the thirteenth century.

John's misappropriation of church revenue meant that for a while church building stood still. The Inderdict which Pope Innocent III laid on England and Wales in 1208 over the Langton affair meant that no church services took place for the next six years. Bells were silent, men who wished to express their faith in the manner to which they had been accustomed found themselves unable to do so. People were depressed on the one hand, but built up an intensity of religious feeling on the other: a combination which helped to change the spirit of church architecture. Even so, it was not until the reign of Henry III (1216–72) that the promise of the Early English style really had the chance to develop.

The church benefited from the tangible appreciation of its grateful followers, and its coffers overflowed. Salisbury Cathedral, the epitome of the age, was built in 40 years, and elsewhere major projects were financed in connection with established abbeys, cathedrals and minsters. The Dominicans came in 1221 and built new churches, as did the Franciscans who arrived three years later. The country was still sparsely populated although the number of people had doubled since the Conquest. More space was needed in the smaller parish churches, but it was religious feeling and not physical necessity which influenced the building of so many churches and enlarging of old ones. The overall result was to provide far more worshipping space than was actually needed; enthusiastic forward planning so to speak. Local styles prove that schools of masons were set up in rural areas where the wealth from the emerging wool trade was coupling with good stone to produce noteworthy architecture.

Thirteenth-century churches were either rectangular or cruciform in **ground plan.** Before the period ended guilds and individuals were building chantry chapels in the angles between chancel and transepts. The square-ended 'lady chapels' which came into being as the most easterly projections

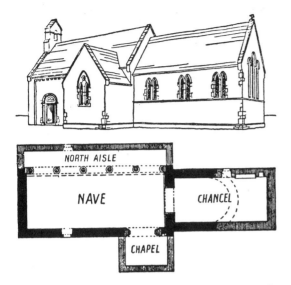

58 *Thirteenth-century additions to the ground plan: aisle chapel and new chancel (scale: 36 feet to 1 inch)*

The great architectural development of the thirteenth century came about because builders began to understand how to deal more effectively with loads and strains. In the vaulting of an oblong area bounded by round-headed arches, the height of diagonal ribs exceeded that of the wall ribs. The pointed arch came about because builders wanted to make the ribs equal in height. They also realised that the thrust from a vaulted roof was concentrated at the corners, and supports placed at these points would resist the outward thrust. The combination of the pointed arch and strategically placed buttresses made for a much firmer structure.

The main feature of early Gothic **mouldings** was the great – and sometimes structurally unsound – depth to which they were undercut. The idea was to accentuate the sharpness of detail against the shadows in the deep hollows behind. It was a short step from the prevalent roll moulding to the pear-shaped or pointed bowtell, made by slightly arching the roll and leaving uncut the arris of the square block from which it was formed. All Gothic mouldings developed from the result, and the thirteenth century proved to be a time of experiment. First the bowtell, pointed and round, took a square-shaped fillet along its leading edge. Then three fillets were set equidistant from each other, as it were, on the upper and lower surfaces as well as at the centre. The fillets were made wider,

next to the chancel, might sometimes have their altars dedicated to the Holy Trinity and not the Virgin. In many places transepts were still being erected as a means of accommodating more people, but being turned into individual chapels as no-one could see the high altar from them or hear what was being said in the chancel. Indeed, as we shall see, the developing relationship between the laity and the clergy was making this something of a problem for all. The importance attached to the celibacy of the clergy occasioned some rethinking of the internal arrangements. The choir and chancel were separated from the nave by a screen at the east end, thus physically emphasising the point of division. Chancels were lengthened to allow more space for the clergy, and given square east ends where they were formerly apsidal. Aisles were low and narrow until c. 1250, when they were widened and heightened and, in larger churches, separated from the nave by tall pillars and pointed arches. Apart from that it was a question of heightening, widening and extending laterally, using the new techniques and features.

59 *Inglesham, Wiltshire. A tiny church with bits and pieces from all periods*

and changed from square to semi-circular in cross section. By the end of the period the scroll moulding was in existence. This was made by cutting a quarter round and one edge of a square fillet and then, instead of completing the fillet, continuing the semi-circle from that point.

In sculpture the accent was on delicacy, moderation and a move towards natural forms which were seen to embody purity. The artists cut deeply and decisively, taking their inspiration from the flora of the countryside although not always applying it in a recognisable form. **Stiff leaf,** for example, was not of any particular type and took its name as much from the erect nature of its stalk as the actual leaf itself. Early leaves hugged the bell of the capital and were widely spaced with deep hollows between, but they were large and not particularly well done. In time the stalks became less important and the several-lobed leaves were crammed tightly together. They were bent and curled, and appeared to grow freely whilst never leaving the plane of the capital.

Perhaps the most enduring and versatile decoration of the period was the **crocket.** It was said to have come from the volutes of classical capitals abroad, but arrived here as a

61 *Uffington, Oxfordshire: a cruciform church built almost entirely in the thirteenth century*

concave hook which edged shafts and gradually took on a foliated or lobed appearance. These little projections included buds, berries, flowers, curled leaves with anything between three and seven lobes, or bunches of foliage. Crisply carved, from the middle of the thirteenth century crockets ran along the sloping sides of canopies, spires, gables, pinnacles, finials, flying buttresses and even hood mouldings. They were placed at regular intervals to be aesthetically pleasing whilst breaking up the background or skyline and – in some cases – affording a hand or foothold for builders.

The art of the sculptor naturally extended to more obvious subjects and we see depicted hawthorn, ivy, oak, maple and columbine.

Dog tooth was particularly popular around arches and in hood mouldings, and was the forerunner of the nail-head decoration of the fourteenth century. It took the form of a quartered pyramid, or a half pyramid, set diagonally to its neighbour and repeated the required length along a hollow moulding. Each raised quarter or tooth could be treated as a leaf, and thus it was an eminently suitable base for the minor decoration of the period.

Chamfers were either flat or slightly hollowed and the **chamfer stops,** the shaped endings to the chamfers, achieved a delicate

60 *Amesbury, Wiltshire: flint fabric with many lancets*

beauty. The moulding ended in a pointed arch style, sometimes trefoiled or to a point. Carved within it might be a leaf form, occasionally separated from the rest of the chamfer by a small roll or hollow across its width. The three-lobed form predominated.

Although vaulting was becoming a feature, **walls** no longer relied on great thicknesses to keep themselves up and support the weight from above. Builders realised the importance of effectively distributing weight and countering thrusts throughout the building. They also realised what was possible in other areas of design if this was properly done. The walls still had a core of rubble, but fresh knowledge enabled them to be built thinner, and to continue in that way throughout the thirteenth century. The stones were cut with greater skill and the tooling was more finely done. The round-headed blind arcade gave way completely to the pointed arch as a decorative feature, and then became trefoil headed. In more advanced cases it was combined with slender shafts and little caps and bases which were characteristic of the period. In larger churches which had a central tower the west end was sometimes treated as a façade, carrying pointed arcades and minor decoration of the day.

Where churches were small and towerless little stone **bell cotes** were often put up at the west end, supported by a system of struts and braces from beneath because the average roof of this period was not constructed to withstand the weight of bells. A buttress, placed centrally down the west wall of the nave, helped to stop the additional weight from pushing it outwards. A similar but usually smaller arrangement was sometimes put up on the east gable of the nave to accommodate the sanctus bell. Some were gabled and decorated with crockets; others had spirelets which were similarly treated. Most held a single bell although some did have double openings.

As walls became thinner it was necessary to help support the stresses placed upon them by increasing the size and effectiveness of buttresses. They had to counter any spreading tendency on the part of the roof which in turn forced out the wall, and so were placed at regular intervals. Builders found that if these were put in the correct positions – and they usually corresponded with the internal bays – comparatively little solid walling was needed between them, and in time the space could be filled by windows. This let more natural light into the church, allowing the play of light and shade which became so important a part of thirteenth-century church planning and is necessary to a good appreciation of Early English interiors. The realisation that walls so treated with buttresses were still

62 *Warmington, Northamptonshire: typically pierced broach spire*

63 *Church Knowle, Dorset: the west tower with pyramid cap*

64 *Felmersham, Bedfordshire: intricate arcading of the west front*

stable undoubtedly helped in the experiments with windows which led to the pointed head filled with tracery.

Early English **buttresses** projected further from the wall than had their predecessors, and usually rose in two or three stages from the ground. They were low and sturdy. Each stage was inclined towards the narrower one above by means of an upward slope, set-off or weathering. The angle of inclination of the set-off was made more acute as it ascended the buttress. The top stage ended in a slope under the cornice, or had a triangular elevation topped by a gable. Occasionally one of those typical little bud-like heads protruded from the underside of the upper gable. Small decorative gables with cusping sometimes rose above little blind arches on the leading surfaces of a staged buttress. Other buttresses of the period were straight-sided with chamfered edges, or else had slender shafts at the angles.

The knowledge that weights tend to concentrate more at the corners of a building, but that the outer thrusts of the arches of a vault meant that the weight had a lateral rather than vertical thrust, led to buttresses being put up at right angles to each other at the junction of two walls. Later, a single buttress enclosed the point at which the walls met and, as clerestories gave height to the

walls, buttresses were placed at regular intervals along their length. In fact the need for buttresses was greatly reduced where a clerestory wall and triforium had been raised over an arcade, as the thrust from any vault was mostly carried down the arches to the ground.

Where churches had tall aisles and nave walls a stone bar, straight along the top and either chamfered or curved on the underside, was fitted between the latter or clerestory and a buttress. This structure was known as a **flying buttress** and was positioned to relieve the thrust from a high vaulted roof. Finding the correct point was a matter of trial and error. Isolated examples occur in thirteenth-century churches, but even at that early period they were sometimes adorned with pinnacles and crockets. Few towers were buttressed, but those used in this way were mostly plain and simple.

Thirteenth-century **string courses** were slight, elegant and ran around the building very close to the features with which they

46

were associated. Their basic level was just below the windows, separating them from the solid wall of the basement below. In contrast to their previous tendency to be interrupted by any obstacle which crossed their path, they now continued right around each feature at the same level, tying it to the main walls. This development is particularly noticeable around buttresses. String courses ran both horizontally and vertically, often continuing over the heads of windows to form identically shaped dripstones. Corresponding strings were carried around the inside of the church.

Timber was still the most common material used throughout in the making of **roofs,** and there the craft of the carpenter was at its most important, although he could not be done without in the centring for arches. To begin with roofs were high pitched and steep, and the width of the aisles beneath was determined by the angle at which the continuous roof sloped. The ridge piece had now come into being, running the length of the apex and tying together the principal rafters. The arrangement below continued to favour the solid tie beam which spanned the area from wall to wall, rested on wall plates, and took the weight of the principal rafters which in turn supported the roof. The tie beam was sometimes carved with the decoration of the day, in particular tooth or embattled ornamentation. Early examples were of approximately the same widths as the walls which supported them.

Extra support was provided by a piece of timber placed vertically between the ridge piece and the centre of the tie beam; this was called a king post. Shorter timbers, called queen posts, were placed between the tie beam and the principal rafters to give even more stability to the roof which, even without any stone vaulting, was still capable of imposing such a weight on the walls below that they might spread outwards. Later roofs were less steeply pitched and the tie beam was dispensed with, leaving the rafters simply trussed. The lean-to, a single slope which adjoined a higher wall, came into fairly common use. Tie beams were also used in support of such roofs and many smaller ones can still be seen spanning the width of aisles. Although some flat boarding took place and many roofs were later lathed and plastered, most roofs put up in the thirteenth century were left exposed from the underside. Occasionally trussed rafter roofs span nave and aisles.

Masons continued to experiment with stone **vaulting,** especially in chancels where although sexpartite vaulting received some attention the quadripartite vault continued to predominate. More ribs were added and they were less massive than before. Together with their moulded lower sections they were completely formed from longer blocks of stone. Complex arrangements produced more if smaller cells between the ribs, and at first these were filled with rubble. Later, ashlar blocks were used. Diagonal ribs ran from corner to corner across the bay of the vault. Subsidiary pairs of short, intermediate ribs, called tiercerons began at the same points as the main supports and met at an angle. They did not cross through the centre of the vault, nor did they complete a continuous line across it. They were often put up abutting, and in conjunction with, transverse ribs set at right angles to the axis of the vault, and the longitudinal ridge rib. All were characteristically moulded and, later in the century, the points at which they met were disguised by bosses which were carved with stiff and natural leaf foliage.

The century was not a great one for **tower** design; many were small and low. But they continued to dominate their surroundings and did not fall down with the frequency of those put up in the preceding century. Most were built at the west end of the church, although some formed the south porch. Changes to the general design of windows meant that belfry openings, especially double ones, could be similarly treated.

As with triforia of the period, the two lancets were sometimes enclosed in a pointed arch. Otherwise pointed arcading continued

47

65 *West Walton, Norfolk: the detached tower*

66 *Bishops Cannings, Wiltshire: large,*
cruciform and almost entirely thirteenth century

the Norman innovation as a decorative feature around the belfry stage of the tower, and was sometimes applied to its lower stage. There were few external stair turrets and if they were lit at all it was usually by single, tiny lancets sometimes trefoil-headed and occasionally gabled. Single lancets were the main source of light in western towers.

Gargoyles made their first appearance, masking a functional necessity. Wherever there was a parapet, water tended to collect behind the stonework. It was released by inserting lead spouts in stone projections and thence through the wall, in order to drain the water from behind. The encasing stonework came, over the centuries, to be one of the great entertainments of church art. But in the thirteenth century they were either left plain or carved with simple grotesques.

During the first half of the century the **spire** developed as an upward extension of the low pyramid with which towers had been capped, and schools of spire builders were established in areas where building stone was good. Where tower and spire were newly built they were designed as a single entity and had no parapet. The stone spire truly 'capped' the tower in as much as it projected slightly at the point of contact and was set on a corbel table. In early examples the spire projected very little from the wall; the corbels were simple double rolls with a deep string course of trefoils and quatrefoils below.

Whilst they directed man's thoughts heavenwards and visually contrasted with the horizontal line of the nave and chancel, spires were really no more than constructional decoration. In fact they were as difficult to build as they were beautiful to look at and embodied the spirit of the age. Stone parapet spires were built, soaring from behind the battlements of existing towers. Some had pinnacles at the corners, decorated with crockets and a finial. They were either square or octagonal in base area, and the builders made the transition from square (or rectangular) tower top to octagonal spire by a device known as a **broach.** This was a half

67 *Long Sutton, Lincolnshire: one of the earliest lead spires*

pyramid of masonry which inclined from each right angle of the tower to a point along each diagonal side of the octagon above supported from within by corner arches called squinches. It was not of a standard height.

The early spires were almost always left plain, as were the diagonal sides throughout the period. Later the cardinal sides were pierced with spirelights, little gabled openings like dormer windows which dimished in size as they ascended the spire. They were purely a decorative feature, to break up the straight line of the spire against the sky, and allowed no significant light to enter.

French glass makers applied their art to the **windows** of some larger churches during the last quarter of the twelfth century, and the vogue spread to the villages. There, a crossbanding of lead provided a kind of windbreak in the openings if they were not otherwise covered. The thick, greyish glass, the grisaille or patterned window with its little floral paintings, had both a decorative and a practical application. Windows needed to be made larger if more natural light was to be allowed into the building, and there needed to be more of them. Glass provided a beautiful way of keeping out the elements and making all this possible, and the **lancet window** which made its appearance early in the thirteenth century, was designed to take it.

The lancet is so called because of its shape which resembles the blade of a knife, although it was evolved to mirror the pointed style of the arches within the church. It began as a single light, generally broad and low, flush with the exterior wall but having a deep internal splay. As the lancet developed through many different sizes during the period, it tended to be wider in the south of the country and taller in the north. From c. 1225 the heads of lancets were frequently treated with projections of masonry, plain or chamfered, known as cusps. The arcs on either side of this feature are called foils, and they ended in either a point or a blunt square tip.

At first single lancets were widely spaced

68 *Early English windows*

with plenty of wall between them. In some cases they were hardly larger than their Norman predecessors, exchanging only a pointed head for the semi-circular. Gradually they increased in size, and the amount of solid wall between them decreased. The whole façade of the church changed and the position of lancet windows became a primary consideration in its design. Many small Norman lights were removed to make way for the larger windows. Lancets were put up in groups of two or three – mostly of the same dimensions as each other – along the east and west walls of transepts and the north and south walls of aisles. Groups of three, five and even seven windows were built in the north and south walls of transepts and above the altar at the east end of the chancel. The group of three was most popular in the latter position, doubtless seen as symbolic of the Holy Trinity. Where the lights in a group were of an uneven number, they were usually stepped upwards towards the centre light, which was increased in width. Otherwise they progressively increased in width from the outside in pairs.

Internally the elements in the group still had deep splays to make maximum use of the light which came through, and the width of the splay might be as much as five times that of the opening. Although from the outside they were obviously set independently in the

wall, the lights seemed almost to be of a piece when viewed from within. When each was separated by slender shafts with little caps and bases, the illusion of embryonic mullions was almost complete.

At first each lancet had its own individual dripstone, although those of a group were connected by short, horizontal string courses. This arrangement created a hollow between them where water collected. The position of the strings was normally determined by the points of spring of the arches in the outer lancets and, as a result, the central dripstone was often stilted. As the lights became taller and the distance between them narrowed, the dripstone was arched above the setting, treating the feature as a whole. The basic shape of windows to come had been formed.

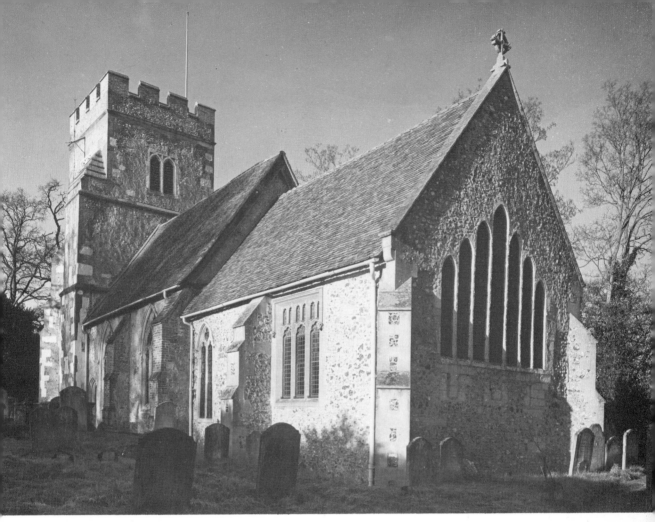

69 *Ockham, Surrey, from the south east*

The next step was to pierce the blank wall between the arched dripstone and the heads of two lancets of equal height with a single, circular opening cut straight through the wall. This formed **plate tracery.** Groups of three stepped lancets were similarly treated, piercing the walls above with circles, ovals and lozenge shapes. Later, these openings were trefoiled or quatrefoiled. After that the thin vertical divisions between the lights were continued upwards, forming a framework of stone mullions and dividing into smaller lights what had now become the head of the window. This is known as **bar tracery.** It began c. 1245 and its simple geometric curves were constructed of separate pieces of stone. In windows composed of lancets below and a circular centrepiece in the head, these features

were often cusped. They were cut out of solid stone in the lower lights but individually inserted into grooves in the sides of the circles, where they stayed in place by mutual pressure. Cusps which are cut out of the inner curve of the arch and not chamfered are a sign of early work, as are those formed of a series of individual circles.

Porches were used for both secular and religious purposes, and so became popular, figuring much more in the design of the church. The first part of the marriage celebration and the service of baptism took place in the large south porches which were deep in relation to their width, high pitched and gabled. They often had vaulted roofs with ribs and bosses, and were externally decorated with square or lozenge diaper

51

work. Large, gallilee porches were set up later in the thirteenth century. The outer openings of porches of the period usually had a dripstone around the head, ending in corbels or stops which took the forms of floral motifs or human heads.

Most south porches which were put up in the thirteenth century protected Norman doorways, for comparatively few were inserted during the later period. In smaller churches they were very plain, pointed or trefoiled and only included a modest amount of dog tooth, stiff leaf or other floral forms on the caps. Some smaller openings such as priest's doorways were square-headed, but doorways generally developed along the same lines as window designs.

The opening years of the century continued the Norman idea of recessed orders with a more slender, cylindrical detached shaft in each nook of the jambs. Now though, the caps and bases were circular with little rolls and dog tooth was the favourite decoration around the pointed head. The thirteenth century also produced the double opening doorway in which the feature was divided into two openings by a slender shaft in the centre, in much the same way as belfry openings had been treated. A double arched doorway appeared in larger churches, whereby two separate arches were built one behind the other and treated quite independently as regards decoration. The wide jamb space between was also quite lavishly decorated and typical arch mouldings throughout were the plain roll, and the pointed or filleted bowtell.

Gable crosses were put up on the roof at the east end of the nave. An abbreviated gable, identical to the east end, was usually built at right angles to it and the cross raised on top facing the east. The basic shape was of a Greek cross, often within or connecting a circle or circular form, the elements of which were occasionally lobed or foliated.

It was the use of the pointed **arch** as a load-bearing feature, coupled with the buttress as a combatant to outward thrusts

which made so much more structurally possible. Some semi-circular arches were built, but the majority became pointed until they were quite acutely so. The flatter segmental arch – one with its centre below the diameter – was also built, as was the equilateral arch which had equal radii and width. Quite early on masons learnt the decorative value of the trefoil-headed arch which was basically formed by placing an open circle or semi-circular arch in the head of a larger one.

An arch is made up of wedge-shaped blocks of stone called voussoirs; the lowest one on each side is a springer and the 'V'-shaped block in the centre of the head is the keystone. In smaller parish churches which did not have sufficient funds or local skill to do otherwise this arrangement – simply chamfered to a lesser or greater degree – sufficed for most of the period. There were rarely more than two or three orders in the arcades, and the arches were low. A common decorative practice of thirteenth-century masons, and one which they frequently applied to chancel arches and to a lesser degree responds (the half pillars at the ends of arcades), was to carry the inner order of the arch onto corbels. They often inserted a shaft with foliated cap and moulded base between the arch and the corbel and in most of these cases the other mouldings were carried right down to the ground. In their decoration, arches were treated quite independently of the piers below them and given dog tooth ornament either on them or forming a hood mould.

The **piers** of country churches were less massive than before. The solid blocks of stone were more skilfully cut, better finished with more sophisticated tools, and fitted more tightly together. Whilst the low, circular pillar continued to be put up in smaller churches three distinct types emerged in the larger ones. There was the central pillar surrounded by a ring of detached shafts, the central pillar with clusters of columns attached, and the pier formed of a cluster of engaged columns. In some clusters, thicker shafts alternated

70 *West Walton, Norfolk: the nave arcade*

with more slender ones. Between 1160 and 1300 there was a vogue for polished stone or marble detached shafts. Narrow rings, called annulets, sometimes ran around the pier at points along its length, apparently tying subsidiary shafts back to the central pillar.

Abaci were no longer square. Some were octagonal and the Early English type was circular with a rounded upper edge. This form began c. 1190 and continued until c. 1360. They had light, moulded edges, deeply undercut to correspond with the hollow in the base.

Capitals were usually circular in plan, moulded and bell shaped. Earlier ones were plain except for rounds and hollows, but as the century progressed stiff leaf foliage spread across the bell. At first it was conservatively done with small, three-lobed leaves on long, stiff stalks. Later five- and seven-lobed leaves and leaf scrolls wended their way around

thirteenth-century capitals and from c. 1280 they grew out of the shaft in a natural manner and took on more recognisable forms. Neither the foliage nor the stalks projected over much and the foliage was nearly always vertical. But in country churches the majority of Early English capitals settled down as a series of concentric rings of varying widths. The capital was divided from the shaft below by an astragal or neck band which was either a narrow, single roll or a fillet of carved ornament.

Bases were circular in essence. They projected much less from the pillar above and began to follow their shapes. The roll mouldings were smaller and c. 1150–1260 a pair of them featured a deep hollow between, known as a water hold. This began to go out of fashion c. 1240 when the rolls were made larger and brought closer together, and the waterhold space was sometimes filled with a

53

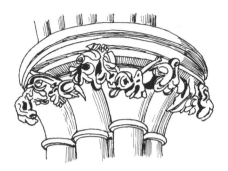

71 *West Walton, Norfolk: capital*

72 *Ivinghoe, Buckinghamshire: capital*

smaller roll. The double or triple roll base came into common use for the rest of the period and the lower one changed from being elliptical to round. The only seats in the church at this time were those in the sedilia for the clergy, and sometimes stone benches against the walls of the aisles for the use of the old and infirm amongst the laity. A projection from the base of a pier sometimes provided more central seating for worshippers.

The **plinth** was no longer a huge block of stone, in some instances no more than a shapeless sarsen. The heavy block first became octagonal with some decorative motif between it and the circular base. In time it took the shape of the base so that the whole pier assumed the same plan.

Piscina and **sedilia** were usually constructed together, and enclosed in the same series of pointed or trefoil-headed arches. Double piscinas became common after

Pope Innocent I announced that the sacred vessels and the priest's hands should not be washed in the same basin. Some included a credence shelf, built into the head of the piscina to hold sacred vessels, cruets, etc., wafers and wine. The seats of the sedilia were stepped downwards towards the west and separated by slender shafts which were sometimes paired. They had characteristic caps and bases with little roll mouldings, and were conservatively decorated with leaves and heads.

Comparatively few **fonts** were made during the thirteenth century because the vast majority of earlier ones continued adequately to fulfil their function. Together with the trend towards less decoration came the sudden, and short lived, fashion for Purbeck and other local shell marbles. These could take a high polish and they made up in brilliance what they lacked in sheer density of sculpture. Marble fonts had square or octagonal bowls which were either quite plain or, more usually, had a shallow arcade of semi-circular, pointed or trefoiled arches. The latter might be pointed or circular trefoils, in single or double rolls. These bowls rested on four slender shafts or else also had a thicker, central stem.

There were even fewer fonts of stone, although the nature of the material allowed much more by way of carving, even within the restricted criteria of the period. The bowls were square, circular, octagonal, cup-shaped and – in some instances – quite bulbous. Some had but a single stem; early supporting

73 *Early English piscina and sedilia*

shafts were detached and later ones were engaged. In essence this followed the evolution of the pier, and the bases and plinths of stone fonts similarly followed the line of each other. Decoration throughout was very much the same as that used on the marble fonts, but the stone bowls also had fleur de lis, vine scrolls, stiff leaf, shells and flowers. The caps on the shafts were sometimes foliated, and the shafts themselves occasionally had a vertical fillet. Font bases were circular or square and in the case of the former sometimes included a water hold moulding.

4
Decorated 1300-1377

THE next period of Gothic architecture, beloved more than any other by the Victorians for its purity and called by them Middle or Second Pointed, corresponded with the first Edwardian era. Church architecture in England parallelled that in France for most of the fourteenth century, but was not similarly to develop into an extremely flamboyant style at the end of it. Here was a weak monarch between the two who epitomised the age of chivalry and pageantry; a time of knights who took their vows before the altar and who gave their heraldry to decorate and enhance the church. There was pomp and splendour to fire the imagination and as religious feeling began to subside, chivalry blended into the services.

More seating was put into the church and the building came in for more secular use than ever before. Plays, festivals, markets, personal business and legal transactions took place within its precincts, and the priests who disagreed with such usage rarely succeeded in getting it shifted further than the churchyard. The walls of the porch were the village notice board and parts of the building were storehouses for parish records and documents. This mainly secular use was entered into by the people with a new, although some might have thought, misplaced enthusiasm. The parish church became wealthy in its own right. Rich landowners, wool and cloth merchants founded chantry chapels where prayers could be said for the continued wellbeing of themselves and their families in life, and the good of their souls when dead. Village vied with village to build a better church and in so doing often obliterated everything which had

gone before. Some were constructed on a scale which had not hitherto been attempted outside monastic or collegiate foundations. New and old buildings were decked with the splendour of the age; heraldic devices, coats of arms and new forms of decoration. The internal walls were full of colour and the services were full of ritual.

The full outcome of the Decorated style was never to be realised. In 1348 came the first touch of bubonic plague known as the Black Death. By 1350 the great wave was spent; in the time between church building and much else had stopped. It is estimated that the plague killed anything up to half of the population, including the clergy, builders, masons and other craftsmen. Many churches remained unfinished until the fifteenth century for, in the wake of the Black Death, there was a scarcity of builders and craftsmen. This showed in several ways. Glasswork, for example, was very much inferior because there were few skilled men left in an art which had never been particularly strong in England. Others moved away from their native areas, so we find isolated examples of local style in unfamiliar territory. And they put a high price on their labour, so many places could not afford to complete work which was begun before the plague. Decorated art went into a short period of transition; men who were still alive had seen death all around, and it sobered them. A great restraint, of which there had been no sign only a few years before, pervaded their work.

Even so the term Decorated is only really true of the largest churches. The more humble village church rarely aspired to the kind of embellishment which is conjured up by the word. There was no great advance in either the plan or execution of church building. It was a period of expansion on the basic plan of aisled nave, chancel, western tower, north and south porch: the most popular type throughout the fourteenth century. Chancels were not usually aisled although they were so widened, and in some cases built so large to accommodate large windows, that they dominated their churches. Otherwise naves and sanctuaries were lengthened, transepts and chapels were added. New aisles were put up parallel with the nave and in some instances they were constructed to extend only to the west wall of a transept. Aisles were put into larger transepts. Strangely enough the polygonal chapter houses which were built on to cathedrals for the purpose of conducting the cathedral's business, and which showed the Decorated achievement at its best, were not in any way applied to the parish church.

Most of the new decoration adorned the exterior. The west face was treated as a façade, with the doorway and traceried window above sometimes enclosed within a deeply recessed arch. Large windows were inserted into the chancel walls, especially at the east end where small windows were also put into the aisles. The internal elevation in large churches was commonly of three storeys: arcade, triforia and clerestory. In smaller ones the middle storey was omitted and the churches were rarely less plain than they had been in the thirteenth century. Triforia became a less important feature in larger churches, diminishing in favour of taller clerestories and higher roofs. Whereas the Early English builders strove for height, their immediate successors seemed to feel they had gone far enough in that direction and applied themselves to widening and opening out. Early English work was austere but creative and although Decorated Gothic was much richer it was a more mature, considered

74 *The fourteenth-century contribution to the ground plan: new aisles, porch, sacristy etc (scale 36 feet to 1 inch)*

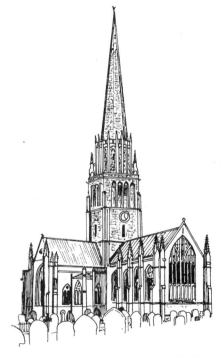

75 *Patrington, Yorkshire: almost wholly of the Decorated period; dominating and beautiful*

76 Bishopstone, Wiltshire. A large, aisleless, cruciform building

richness which harmonized with the genuine feeling of the times.

From c. 1330 a massive programme of church building took place, but one which more than at any other period showed the quality of English workmanship at its two extremes.

Fourteenth-century **mouldings** were numerous but much less deeply undercut than they had been. Early rolls were small; they increased in size with the years and the hollows between became broader. The bowtell and triple fillet continued to be a favourite although the side fillets were frequently broader than the central one. By removing the projections and flattening the bowtell, the masons produced a beautiful form known as a **wave moulding,** an undulation which could be either gentle or severe depending on the depth or angle of the hollow on either side in relation to the convex curve. Pairs of wave mouldings with alternating hollows were a common feature.

The **ball flower** born out of the Early English dog tooth and of which it was basically a rounded form, was profusely employed throughout the period. It resembled a three-lobed ball, as it were a flower with petals incurved upon a central bead. But there were variations; some of the globes were pierced with three or four linked holes. Occasionally they appeared in conjunction with **four-petalled flower** or diaper flower, another favourite of the period which often occupied a parallel hollow in, for example, arch moulding. Here the four outward curving leaves from a central bead formed a square. The device was particularly used in cornices.

Crockets really came into their own, but the stiff, incurved style gave way to naturalistic foliage. Large floral forms swept up sloping sides towards equally flamboyant finials at the top.

Whilst sculptors went in for naturalistic foliage elsewhere, sometimes inhabited by insects, birds and animals, there was also a great vogue for carving human heads out of

77 Compton Beauchamp, Oxfordshire. A small, downland church of chalk

58

78 *Heckington, Lincolnshire, from the south west*

79 *Edington, Wiltshire: Decorated and Perpendicular styles*

corbels and this was exquisitely done. Likenesses of kings and their queens were favoured; bishops, wimpled ladies and the working man supported roofs and arches all around the church and were put up as label stops on the outside.

Interior **walls** continued to be decorated in colour, but as the surfaces were not well prepared very little of this work has survived. The dressed blocks of stone on the outside were generally larger and longer in relation to their height. Tooling was finely done and the stones fitted very tightly together.

The **ogee arch** was developed in the fourteenth century as a decorative feature, and then applied as widely as possible. The shape can be defined as a continuous, flowing double curve which is concave above and convex below and springs from two opposing radii. Because the head of an ogee arch takes the form of two reversed curves, the feature cannot withstand heavy loads, and so does not appear in nave arcades, chancel arches or in any primarily structural way. About 1300 the ogee canopy began to replace its straight-sided predecessor, and within a very few years we see it in doorways and window tracery as well as forming their hood mouldings or dripstones; in tombs, easter

sepulchres, cusping, mouldings, niches, sedilia and piscina, decorative arcading and on buttresses. A depressed ogee was sometimes a feature of window tracery, set beneath a pointed arch. What makes the feature even more obvious are the variations available on the theme and the minor decoration which could be included in it. The upper curves and lower curves could vary in length within their pairs, and they might be depressed or acute. The arch itself came in for cusping and it was often framed by crockets, foliage, ball flower, etc., terminating at the apex in a pinnacle with crockets and finial.

Chamfers did not escape the unmistakable undulations of the ogee curve although many were still plain and flat. They sometimes ended in a triangular shape but by far the most popular stop of the Decorated period was a trefoil or quatrefoil; sometimes cusped and with eyes, and occasionally enclosed within an ogee arch.

Buttresses achieved their fullest development as regards both decoration and pleasing proportions. Pairs of identical corner buttresses, placed diagonally at the point where two walls met but not enclosing the angle became a characteristic feature. So too, did the practice of putting up a single support

80 *Whitbourne, Herefordshire, a typical country church, built of large blocks of stone*

81 *a Ball-flower*

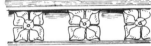

b Four-leafed decoration

at an angle of 45°, enclosing the point at which two walls met. Both of these types were occasionally used in conjunction and applied to a tower. There the angle buttress rose above the point at which the heads of two similarly designed diagonal buttresses died into the walls, partly resting on the set-offs and otherwise corbelled out from the wall.

Buttresses were wider than before, had a greater projection at the base but were still commonly built in two – and sometimes three – stages with either set-offs or string courses between. Often both were included, the string course of the wall being carried around the buttress at the same level below a set-off. Sometimes a string course, running close beneath a window, takes a sudden vertical dive in order to continue horizontally around a buttress at a more suitable level.

Many buttresses were plain but for the chamfered arris, yet derived considerable beauty from their splendid proportions. They had bases which were either plainly chamfered or heavily moulded and the structure terminated at the head with the upper weathering inclined into the wall. The width of the weathering sometimes exceeded that of the surface of the buttress. Otherwise triangular or gable-shaped heads were a

feature of the period, the latter completed by a trefoiled ridge or topped with a finial. When decoration was sparse it was mostly confined to the upper stage where there might be trefoiled panels or a niche, perhaps itself trefoiled, cusped or set within an ogee head. Niches were often canopied and decorated with crockets and a finial. Where these or panels appeared on the face or sides of buttresses they were often delicately done, the latter including tracery. Sometimes the head of a buttress ran through battlements above when the opportunity might be taken to include a small niche at the point. Pinnacles were rarely used on buttresses of this period.

String courses were commonly scroll mouldings or some variation with an ogee as its lower curve, all delicately done to produce a graceful outline. In the majority of cases a square fillet still formed the leading edge, and any hollows were always on the underside.

Roofs continued to be mostly built of timber and were covered with either stone roofing tiles, lead or wood shingles. Builders had a better appreciation of the ways in which roofs should be supported and the effects of various structural arrangements, so that more consideration was given to visual effect and decoration. One method which served both

61

was to camber the tie-beam. This helped to counter the additional loads from above imposed by more sophisticated roofing systems which might otherwise have caused it to sag. The tie-beam was often moulded or carved with minor decorations of the day, and it could be supported from beneath by arched braces which sometimes met in the centre.

A similar arrangement formed the arch-braced roof (see figure 97 page 76); a brace with a continual internal curve was set between the purlin and the ridge piece where it met another making a continuous curve. The thrust of the braces was relieved by wall posts beneath the principal rafters, which in turn prevented the roof from spreading. Another step in this direction was made by the insertion of a horizontal timber, known as a collar, between the principal rafters near their highest point.

Vaulting was done in wood, but rarely, and in stone, although there was very little of either after the middle of the century. Beautifully carved **bosses** were put up wherever possible at the intersection of ribs: intricate knots of foliage which helped to promote a continuous effect by hiding the joins of the ribs. And there were more of these. The quadripartite vault continued to be popular although in the south and west of the country short lierne ribs crossed from one boss to another, producing a very effective star-like shape and leading to some extremely complicated arrangements (see figure 100 page 79).

It was not until this period, and even then none too soon in most areas, that full advantage began to be taken of the **clerestory,** and it became a standard feature. Town churches, and then the smaller village ones,

82 *Patrington, Yorkshire: interior*

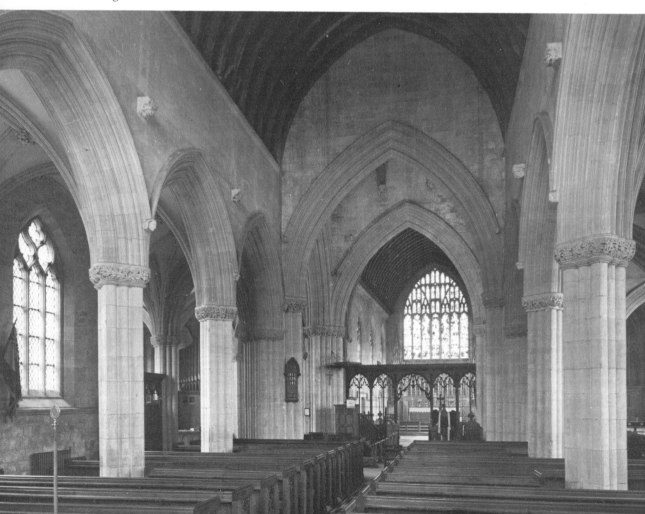

followed the example of the cathedrals. In larger buildings clerestory windows had the more conventional arched heads and were as tall as the depth of the feature allowed and as wide as they could be without being out of proportion. Some had two-light windows in each bay. The most common arrangement elsewhere was a row of small, single lights which could be either circles, squares, spherical triangles, trefoils, quatrefoils or sixfoils. Sometimes different shapes were mixed, and the lights often included cusping.

Until the fourteenth century **parapets** were rarely added and were either plain chamfered above and carried on corbels, or treated very simply with minor decoration. The Decorated period developed this feature to its complete state of coping, parapet wall and cornice or string course for its artistic value in joining large individual features such as buttresses and pinnacles. These broke up the building and occasionally burst into the skyline. Pinnacles were still rare, so such features tended to concentrate in certain areas and were not applied overall to buildings, and a method of cohesion was necessary. By the end of the period the embattled parapet had come into being.

The cornice often included ball flower, wandering four-leaf decoration or small heads. The parapet wall was pierced with trefoils, quatrefoils, flowing tracery or an openwork representation of the four-leaf motif. A favourite form was the trefoil contained within a triangle which was sometimes alternately inverted. Parapets applied to the sloping sides of roof gables were particularly beautiful, and they often included niches at the points where they ran over the heads of features such as windows, into whose dripstone the niche might also be incorporated.

Although some octagonal **towers** were put up, the two-, three- or four-stage square plan western tower continued to be favoured. Some were remarkably plain and un-buttressed, but this was unusual. Angle or diagonal buttresses now ascended into pinnacles beyond the parapet, and helped to increase the appearance of solidity in a feature which was most probably larger in base area than at any previous time. In many cases the buttresses were ornamented, and those which did not continue into pinnacles at least rose the full height of the tower.

Octagonal stair turrets were for the first time considered as an integral part of tower design, and were consequently better proportioned. Where fairly large lights existed in the upper stages of the tower the presence of a stair turret sometimes meant some compromise in the arrangement of the windows on that face. Turret lights were tall and narrow; elongated lancets began the period, but they were later to have the depressed ogee head or were ornamented with small amounts of foliage and tracery. Base mouldings were deep and done with a strength of purpose. Many were panelled.

Belfry openings were either single two-light windows with traceried heads in each face of the tower, or pairs of two-lights with a quatrefoil in the head. These lights were not glazed, but the fourteenth century saw the introduction of sound holes to allow ventilation into the ringing loft: an all-over arrangement of small holes pierced through solid masonry.

Much steeple building took place in the fourteenth century. The builders strove, not always successfully, to complement tower with spire and strike the right proportional balance between them. Just as the majority of octagonal towers were put up during this period, so too was an octagon sometimes provided between the top of a square tower and the base of an octagonal spire. **Spires** were built in stone where that material was available and otherwise, particularly in the south east, of oak, leaded timber or shingles. The broach continued to be popular in either material, but was made smaller. It was gradually superseded by the spire which soared from behind a parapet. Occasionally broaches were replaced by square or octagonal angle pinnacles, and we find various combinations of broach, parapet and pinnacle.

By far the most common form of parapet spire in the villages had neither broach nor pinnacle and struck a sharp contrast with both tower and skyline. This was sometimes relieved by ribs (slender roll mouldings). Ball flower or crockets rushed up the ridges. Horizontal banding was rare as this detracted from the height. The spire had a smaller base area and was slender, with perhaps a slight entasis so that the sides would not seem to be concave. The angle buttresses of the tower were continued above the parapet and topped by pinnacles which were virtually spirelets. These visually carried the transition from tower to spire in place of broaches. The next step was to throw flying buttresses from the base of the pinnacles to the sides of the spire.

Windows were now to become the most distinguishing feature of the church in both number and size, in proportion to the available wall space. Although some of the heads were wide and acutely pointed most of the smaller ones were obtuse and in some cases square-headed. Not only was the tracery to burst out of its geometrical confines into wild and intricate flowing forms, but each type was to achieve a great variety and in many cases geometrical and flowing figures were described in the same window.

83 *Higham Ferrers, Northamptonshire: the east end*

The fourteenth century began by continuing the early English arrangement of two lights with simple bar tracery framed by intersecting mullions continued into the head, plain or cusped. **'Y'-tracery** was formed when a single mullion divided into two branches of equal length within the head. When more than one mullion in the same window was similarly treated, **intersecting tracery** resulted forming lancets below and lozenge shapes in the head. Even at this point bar tracery was fully developed with a considerable number of different shapes and designs in the head. These shapes were called **geometrical tracery** because of the precise way in which geometrical figures such as circles, lozenges, curvilinear and equilateral triangles, etc. were described in the head where they recurred, and were often combined. The more lights there were to a window the more lavish could be the treatment of the heads. Windows in quite small churches of the period had up to four lights and there were as many as nine in the larger buildings. Central lights were sometimes narrower or taller than their fellows, occasionally running right through the head. Tracery bars sometimes diverged upwards and outwards from the central light, resembling the head of the window arch inverted, and enclosing a circle – itself filled with tracery. The circle was the favourite figure of the time and was central in the head of the window, usually segmented or subdivided by small but similar geometrical figures. These also appeared elsewhere in the window where they were no longer bounded by circles as in earlier tracery. A long-lobed, pointed trefoil was introduced initially where the confining arch was more acute, but rapidly spread throughout the head as a general feature of later geometrical work. Dagger decoration, shaped like a spearhead, internally cusped and arched, also became a characteristic of Decorated window tracery. In small churches the central figure was more likely to be a trefoil or quatrefoil.

In **Kentish tracery** the main figure is a four pronged star-like shape, beautifully done, and which bears closer inspection. In fact it is formed of four elongated trefoils, set diagonally, and is cusped with small projections curving into the centre of the light.

One big drawback to geometrical tracery was that there were usually odd shapes left over which had to be glazed with difficulty. Glass was becoming more plentiful. Artists were getting to the stage where they wanted to fill their windows with colourful glass, not only depicting saints and biblical characters but foliage as well. Also the window, however complicated, was composed entirely of individual pieces which never quite gave up their individual autonomy. Ogee arches and flowing curves broke away from this. **Reticulated tracery** appeared early in the transition of geometrical to curvilinear which was to produce fine flowing forms. It was done by elongating circles into ogee shapes and repeating them in a honeycomb pattern which completely filled the head. The style needed at least three lights with ogee arches as heads, similarly continued until they met the window arch. The rich effect of reticulated tracery is more overpowering as the number of lights below increases. The next logical step was to give the ogee heads of the lower lights a sharper point and slightly change the vertical ogee shapes above to form **flamboyant tracery.** This was done, though rarely in this country, but taken to its extremes in France to correspond in essence with the rectilinear tracery of the English Perpendicular period.

In this country **flowing tracery** was developed by dispensing with the circular and ogee shapes and allowing the tracery to branch off into undulating curves of exceptional beauty in which the mouchette predominated. This was a curved spear-head, cusped and arched on the inside. It was particularly effective when used as

the segments of a circular or wheel window – which were more numerous in the fourteenth century – since it gave the illusion of movement. In flowing tracery the forms blended together and provided an almost infinite number of decorative possibilities. Many windows which had rich tracery also had mullions and jambs which were plainly chamfered. Otherwise · they might be richly moulded and studded in hollows there and in the tracery by ball flower, sometimes in conjunction with the Early English nail-head motif, forming a rich

84 *Leominster, Herefordshire: geometrical tracery with ball-flower encrustation*

profusion of decoration. Pairs of lights in a larger window were often enclosed in a sub-arch whose jambs were not those of the window, thereby forming a head above the two lights. This might be treated independently with tracery. Many mullions had shafts with characteristically moulded caps and bases.

Porches were not numerous, but were fairly plain, with high pitched roofs and exterior openings of similar design to the interior door-ways. Some had parapets and they might also be decorated with heraldry. Others were built with upper rooms in which parish records and documents could be safely kept, and parish meetings took place.

During this period a number of openwork timber porches were put up, built on stone or wooden bases. These were usually gabled with arch braces, and bargeboards which were frequently carved. Doorways were moulded and pointed, surrounded by elements of window tracery in woodwork.

The detached shaft was gradually abandoned throughout the church, and although there seemed more of a reluctance to dispense with it in **doorways** the early fourteenth century saw its demise. Doorways varied in size and were mostly pointed with their jambs chamfered at an angle of 45°. Arch mouldings were either carried on the same plane as engaged shafts or were continued down the jambs without caps and, in many instances, without bases. In well moulded arches of two orders we find the pointed arch framing a non-structural trefoil-headed or ogee shape, which might be cusped, and even above that there might be a straight-sided or ogee-shaped gable or hood mould either plain or enriched with crockets and ending in the customary finial.

The doorway was often surmounted by a niche which was sometimes included within the gable. As the style progressed so did the abundant use of crockets and foliage; the latter especially of a large three-lobed fleshy leaf type, decorated the spandrels of doorways. Floral motifs and the customary ball flower

decorated hood mouldings and the hollows between arch mouldings. Where the hood moulding was carried above stops these were usually leafy, but in keeping with the pageantry of the times, they were often carved as the heads of kings and queens.

The **doors** were themselves constructed of vertical planks of oak, now banded in two places by richly ornamented iron work, with leafy designs later in the period. Rich tracery, reticulated and flowing, was carved on the door. The smaller doorways such as priest's doors, and those to stair turrets might be pointed, square-headed or ogee-d, in which case the depressed ogee was a favourite. Jambs, shafts, etc. very much followed the pattern of the main doors but were plainer, and the pieces did not have the elaborate heads to be found elsewhere. Priest's doors had more decoration and were sometimes canopied.

In smaller churches the **pier** was a plain simple affair with either a cylindrical or octagonal pillar which sometimes had a vertical fillet from cap to base. The latter were similarly shaped and moulded. Elsewhere the various types of thirteenth-century compound piers gave way to four or eight cylindrical shafts, diamond-shaped in plan. Fillets were sometimes used on all the shafts of the former, and where there were eight in the cluster thin and thicker shafts alternated. Any hollows in this arrangement tended to be small but deep.

The **abacus** now became the upper moulding of the capital where it was carved from the same block of stone, but still had a hollow or quirk beneath. The capital itself, although narrower, was a combination of scroll and roll mouldings, ogee-shapes and fillets which remained of fairly standard design for the whole of the period.

Occasionally capitals were omitted, or else there was no astragal at the neck. They were otherwise circular and either moulded or the bell was covered with naturalistic foliage. This term was applied to carvings which in type, shape and form emulate actual works of

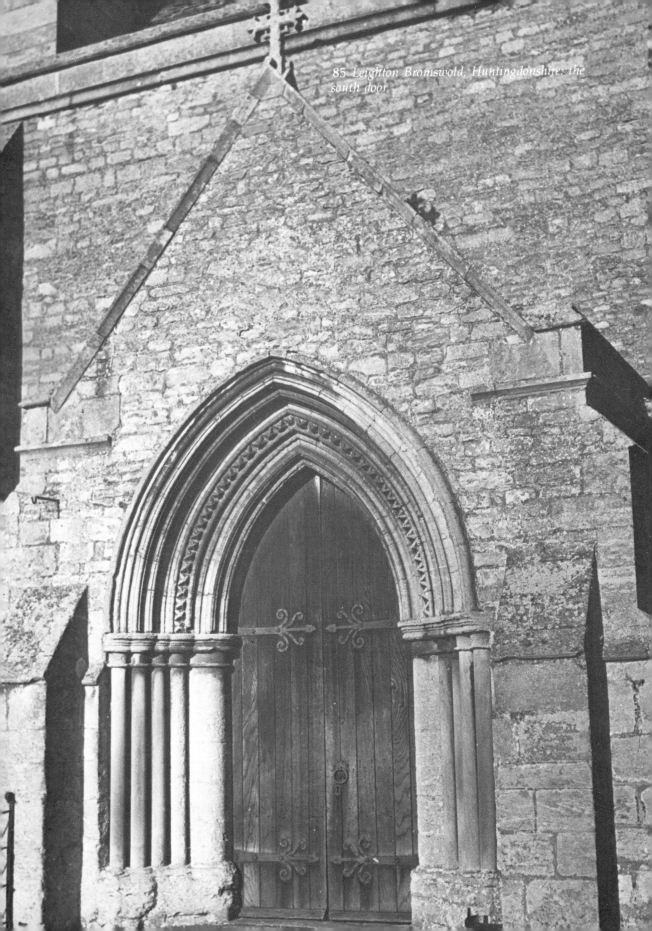

85 *Leighton Bromswold, Huntingdonshire: the south door*

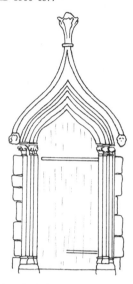

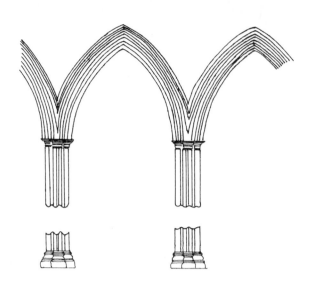

86 *Ogee-headed doorway*

87 *Decorated piers, arches and bases*

nature to the best of the carver's ability. It contrasted with the stylistic and undefined flora which had gone on before, and was exquisitely done. The carver paid particular attention to the finish, working to a smooth surface the underside and the back of the work if it stood away from the capital. Little human heads were sometimes carved amidst a surfeit of ivy, oak, berries, fir cones, maple and hawthorn. Yet the idea of leaves on long stalks as if growing out of the shaft below was abandoned, and in its place leaves were grouped on twigs which made no pretence of live growth. Gradually the leaves increased in size and in many instances stalks of any kind were omitted so the leaves appeared simply to adhere to the capital. Later a bulbous and unnatural curve occurred in even naturalistic foliage, simulating the opposing undulations of the popular ogee shape. Sometimes there was a gap between the foliage on the bell and the astragal beneath, whilst the latter was commonly a scroll moulding.

Bases were deeper, showing a new importance in keeping with what was going on around the exterior of the church. At first they were formed of two or three rolls with decorative mouldings in the hollows, but the lowest moulding had a flat underside. Later it

comprised mainly reversed ogee shapes and wave mouldings, and closely followed the line of the pillar above.

Plinths could be in several stages, round, square or octagonal. They were generally smaller in base area than before, thereby losing some of their prominence to the base. Generally speaking, non-constructional arches were richly ornamented and cusped. They contained a considerable amount of foliage with grotesque and human heads peeping out from between the leaves. Hood mouldings tended to soar high above the feature or else canopied heads ended in elaborate finials.

Constructional **arches,** on the other hand, continued to be plain and pointed, although the latter to a lesser degree than in the previous century. Chancel arches which had come in for so much embellishment were now of two or three orders, plainly chamfered, and were either supported by engaged piers or continued to the ground.

Fixtures such as sedilia, piscina, easter sepulchres, niches and tombs were at their richest. They were given carved stone canopies, many of which had the characteristic ogee shape, and were decorated with crockets, ball flower, and finial. The

68

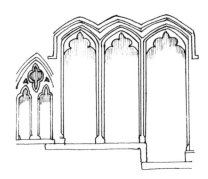

88 *Decorated piscina and sedilia*

double piscina went out of fashion and the piece was treated independently of carved effigies rested on their tombs with their feet on little dogs, and surrounded by crests and heraldic devices.

With few exceptions which tended to be variations on the unmounted tub shape or mounted basin and goblet shapes, **font** bowls were octagonal and stood on similarly shaped shafts. Gone was the fashion for polished marble with its simple arcading, and the conservatively carved freestone. In poorer villages the faces of the font bowls were left plain but for rim and base mouldings, and occasionally supporting heads were corbelled out from the shaft. The supports were sometimes given an inward curve and might be divided by strings.

The ogee, coupled with a desire to treat all faces of the bowl and support in the same way, at once meant a very rich design. Such arches, cusped and crocketed with finials and with floral motifs in the spandrels were carved over shallow niches. At first untenanted, they were later given the likenesses of saints or biblical scenes. Straight-sided gables were often carved on each face, crocketed on the outside, foiled and cusped within. The other main type of decoration was window tracery which showed flowing forms as the main panel design, and trefoils or quatrefoils in the spandrels and on the shafts.

On more ornate examples the sides of the bowl were divided by either buttresses or shafts, which were topped by pinnacles. The

89 *Brailes, Warwickshire: font, early fourteenth century*

bases of these were often supported on heads or knots of foliage which were either corbelled out of the surface of the bowl or the underside, or set on the base moulding.

69

5
Perpendicular 1377-1547

THE fifteenth century saw the fruition of a style which was peculiarly English. No period of architecture lasted as long as Perpendicular, had more local variations reflected in such a variety of individual features, or so defied generalisation. In parish churches it was executed by masons who were not the best but who could cope with its simple lines. They produced elegant, well proportioned buildings. The name Perpendicular is derived from the way in which rigid, vertical mullions were carried straight into the head of the window without any tendency to diverge above the springing of the arch. The basic straight, vertical line was employed throughout the building. For the most part this style seems plain when compared with fourteenth-century work, and church interiors are considered to be cold. Yet, as we shall see, the style allowed for inspired exuberance in local decoration and individual features.

Masons envisaged and planned their churches as a whole, paying particular attention to spaciousness and light. The shape of shade, shadow and light was no longer a question of sculptured detail and the interest lost in this area was applied to the overall contrasts afforded by large windows and high walls.

It is important to understand that the shell of the church had become the setting for a number of dominant features which were reaching their peak of creative excellence. Like any work of art, they were best seen either in a plain setting or in juxtaposition to uncluttered surroundings. An example of this might be a profusion of fan vaulting seemingly bursting

within the confines of a small chapel as viewed through the vertical austerity of the nave arcade. Also, there was the amazing rise of the woodworker, whose art was now on an equal footing with that of the mason. No longer was timber simply a means of bracing; it had come down into the nave.

The masons' rectilinear tracery and other decoration could be matched in decorative woodwork. Soon carpenters were to work hand in hand with painters, covering the fine oakwork with bright colours.

Voluntary organisations known as parochial or religious gilds came about to provide community services in the fourteenth century. They were joined by craft gilds: powerful and rich trading associations. These either built their own chapels, or took over some part of the church, effecting no structural change whilst admitting several screened-off chapels under the same roof. This was done by the use of parclose screens; carved, decorated and painted woodwork, often panelled below but with openwork lights above. The squint or hagioscope – a rectangular opening through the wall or pillar between an aisle and the chancel – was necessary in order to see the main altar and synchronise what was there taking place with events in a chapel.

This was a time of building financed by the parish and the people who wanted to temper their religion with colour and comfort. Seating, which had been introduced in the fourteenth century, became common and plain-ended benches gave way to finely carved, panelled and traceried examples. In the west country they remained

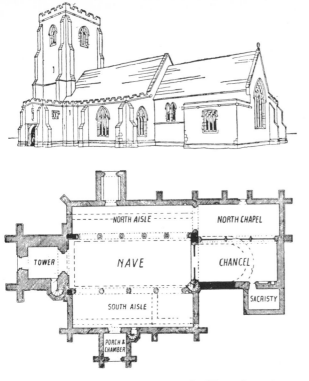

90 *Ground plan showing early fifteenth-century extensions: tower, porch, nave and chancel aisles etc (scale 36 feet to 1 inch)*

nave aisles. In some places desirous of keeping the cruciform character of the church, aisles were added and enlarged but the transept was also heightened and lengthened. Otherwise a north chapel was frequently the first to be built, later followed by one to the south. The parish sometimes undertook the building of a fine western tower. This effectively destroyed the chance of the sort of façade in the true sense of the word, which one finds in the larger churches. Their substitute was the way in which the tower generally – or at least its western face – was decorated.

A rich landowner might add a north porch where it was more convenient for him to enter and leave the church, and a two-storey porch might appear on the south side. Chapels

square-ended, but elsewhere were of the shaped shoulder variety which had poppy heads and other foliage and figures, all delicately carved. In many instances the backs of the benches were also carved. The **plan** of the church was influenced by the requirements of gilds and individuals for chapels and chantries. These were structurally accommodated by extending the nave aisles eastwards to end flush or nearly so with the east wall of the chancel, so that the basic ground plan became a rectangle. The chancel was separated from its aisles by a low arcade of one or two bays and occasionally the opportunity was taken to add a clerestory. A 'three gabled' arrangement occurred when the aisles were gabled to the same height as the nave.

Cruciform churches, especially those with small transepts, could be made rectangular by building chancel aisles to the same width as the transept and similarly widening existing

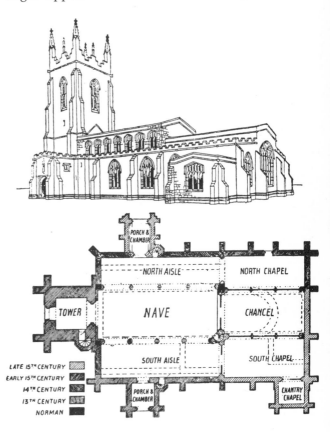

91 *The late fifteenth-century final transformation: clerestory, chapels, etc (scale 36 feet to 1 inch)*

71

sprung up immediately to the east of porches. In smaller churches the south aisle and arcade were often rebuilt, and everywhere aisle roofs were lowered. In fact all roofs became flatter and tended to disappear behind parapets.

Internally, the triforium became a stretch of blank wall. Sometimes its position was marked by a course of panel work, but mostly a narrow string course alone divided the clerestory from the arches below. Nave walls which had succumbed to the thrust from the roof above and were leaning outwards, were taken down and rebuilt to include a clerestory. This became a standard feature of Perpendicular churches.

There was a wide range of surface **decoration.** String courses were sometimes omitted from smaller village churches; otherwise they were angular with wide and shallow hollows. Some were bands of quatrefoiled panels. Carved motifs and devices which had been born at the height of heraldry were now included within the vogue for panel work which had spread from the windows to the walls. This found particularly fine expression in basement mouldings. Square panels of stone tracery were designed around a single motif as a centrepiece. Foliage was stylised or bulbous and undulatory.

There was less of it and recognisable forms were often put together in an unnatural shape. Parapets commonly included bands of quatrefoiled panels as well as brattishing – delicately carved openwork. Trefoils, quatrefoils or multifoils headed the arches in the rectilinear-style panels. These were usually cusped. Cornices, labels, cresting, took on roses, vine and strawberry leaf. There, and in the spandrels, were to be found the emblems of saints, heraldic shields, armorial bearings and badges, beasts and birds.

The square four-leaved flower predominated, later to give way to the Tudor rose and portcullis. Canopied niches with statues appeared within and without, and tiers of statues in the form of a reredos often occupied much of the interior east wall. Pulpits, stalls, screens, tombs, fonts, etc. were adorned with other structural and decorative features in miniature such as vaulting, buttresses, battlements and pinnacles.

Dripstones or label stops were frequently no more than horizontal rectangles at right angles to the moulding, returned at the springing of the arch. Occasionally they were curved towards the wall and embattled, or with a single decorative motif in the hollow. A

92 *St Cleer, Cornwall.*
The church is built in
granite and its proportions are
typical of the far west

93 *Lanreath, Cornwall. Built almost entirely in*
the Perpendicular period

common treatment of the label at this point was to return it in a circle, square, diamond shape or octagon, enclosing a centrepiece which might be a single tudor rose, four-leaved flower or monogrammed shield.

Walls were high, constructed of skilfully wrought ashlar, but weakened in themselves by the extent to which the surface area was reduced to a minimum in order to accommodate large windows. The blocks were more uniform in size and finely tooled. Areas which had little or no freestone might use flint, and a considerable brick trade – first employed to any extent in the thirteenth century – had now become established. Water fell clear of the walls below by continuing the slope of higher pitched roofs onto wide eaves. Otherwise, as parapets became an important and effective feature so too did a variety of gargoyles; the water which collected as it ran off the lower lead roofs was released through spouts. The actual channel behind the parapet came to rest over any corbels, thus pushing forward the whole parapet beyond the line of the wall below. With the Tudors came the invention of the down pipe. But sculptors had so much fun with gargoyles that even where they were not employed, grotesques which served no functional purpose continued to be put up.

Battlements soon ousted the horizontal parapet, and a great variety of embattled parapets came into being. Early ones were solid, but ornamental. Gradually the merlons (the raised sections as opposed to the spaces between which are called embrasures and only of material significance when the feature appears on a fortification) came to be pierced with panel-shaped openings or were similarly carved. Trefoil or quatrefoil designs were popular; so too were the square and four-leafed flower. Some openwork was multifoiled. It is a common fallacy that the width of a merlon is the same as the space between two. Many are similar but, especially in the highly decorated ranges, one must look

94 Cullompton, Devon: the tower

for optical illusions. Parapets were properly constructed in three parts: coping, band and cornice, all of which were richly ornamented. Coping, which had hitherto continued all around the battlements became generally confined to the horizontal edges. It is common to find a blank band beneath richly carved or open-work battlements. In some cases the decoration of the merlon was extended the whole depth of the parapet and the masonry between also richly treated. In such instances where the coping was continued around the battlements as a continuous piece, the decoration on the panels between was continued below the width of the coping on either side. Openwork merlons were often put up with carved panels between.

One of the results of thinner walls and less solid masonry between the windows was the need to make the slender **buttresses** project still further from the surface of the walls. Even the magnificent Perpendicular churches of East Anglia rarely have non-tower buttresses which exceed two stages, and such were generally uncommon although walls were higher. Masons saw them as a framework for the windows and accordingly embellished them with niches, quatrefoils, panelwork, etc. The upper stage was either inclined into the wall some way below the parapet or continued through it by means of a shaft topped by a pinnacle. In many instances diagonal buttresses completed the right angles of aisle walls, whereas larger pairs were put up at right angles to each other in support of the east end of the chancel.

Diagonal buttresses climbed the tower and corresponded with its stages, tending to die into the wall just below the parapet. Another technique was to build tower buttresses at right angles to each other on abutting wall surfaces but set a little way equidistant from the corner. In this type they commonly terminated some way below the parapet, and often about half way up the top stage of the tower. Particularly in the west country the uppermost set-off – and in some cases all of them – was continued upwards by a pinnacle

95 *Northleach, Gloucestershire. One of the great 'wool' churches of the Cotswolds*

on a slender shaft. Yet another variation was to fill the angle at which corner buttresses met with a diagonal projection for some way along its length, topped by a pinnacle.

Flying buttresses never achieved particular popularity in this country. One may sometimes see where a few have been put up and the intention, never realised, was to build others. Occasionally they were put up along the whole length of the nave.

In the far west of the country unbroken aisles ran the length of the church. Their **roofs,** as those of the nave and chancel, were treated as single expanses with the characteristic **barrel or wagon** arrangement. This was composed of curved, slightly pointed principals seated on the wall plate and rising to the ridge piece. Rafters followed the lines of the principals, and purlins joined them at intervals. The points of intersection were marked by carved bosses. The square panels which resulted might be boarded or plastered, but in some instances the evidence of rich carving on members which would then be hidden indicates that this was not necessarily the original intention.

Everywhere the talents of carpenters and woodcarvers turned into a major source of beauty, to be painted or gilded. The craftsmen's chance came as many old roofs

96 *Long Melford, Suffolk, from the south east*

were destroyed in making clerestories. Every kind of openwork timber roof was put up with particular emphasis on trussed rafter and king post arrangements, and tie-beams supported by braces. The principals were connected a short distance from the ridge by a horizontal collar beam which had an upwards camber in some roofs; sometimes they were supported by carved braces. Most of the members were richly carved.

The most beautiful roofs were those which were open, giving the appearance of height and spaciousness; this had come about with the removal of the tie-beam. The **hammerbeam roof** is almost exclusive to the eastern countries. It has as its base horizontal posts which project into the church and support arch braces. The latter reduce the width of the span and therefore the outward thrust on the walls below. Hammerbeams were richly moulded or carved, abutted a similarly treated cornice and were raised above wall posts which also helped to reduce the thrust from above. It was customary to place a carved angel with outspread wings on the end of each hammer beam, and to colour

or gild them. The bases of wall plates were similarly treated with corbelled-out angels. Where one tier of hammer beams was raised above another and connected to it by a curved bracket the result was a **double hammerbeam roof,** and such are the richest and most highly decorated in the country. Even the spandrel of the bracket beneath each hammerbeam was elaborately traceried.

The best and most complicated **vaulting** was done during this period even though it was comparatively rare. It appeared mainly in porches which had upper chambers, and sprung from the walls beneath towers, above aisles and chantry chapels. Not a great deal was done because timber was less costly than stone and the standard of woodwork and carving was so good. Lierne ribs continued to be popular and to increase in number, resulting in some extremely complicated designs.

But it was a peculiarly English form of decoration, known as the **fan vault,** for which this type of work in the fifteenth century was famed. It may be described as a trumpet-shaped, inverted cone of masonry

75

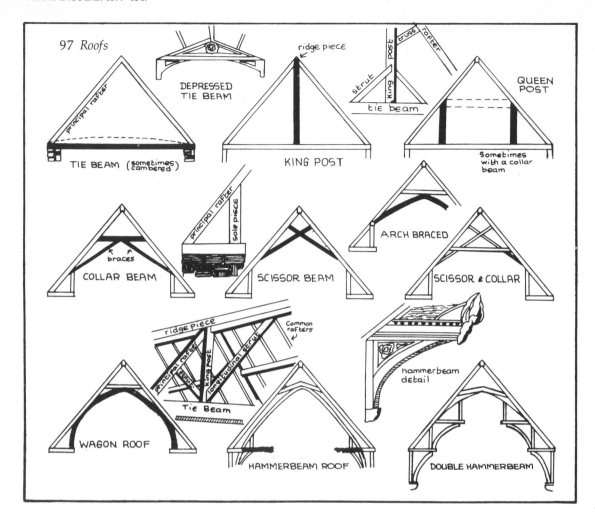

97 Roofs

DEPRESSED TIE BEAM

ridge piece

principal rafter

QUEEN POST

TIE BEAM (*sometimes cambered*)

KING POST

Sometimes with a collar beam

strut

king post

truss rafter

tie beam

braces

COLLAR BEAM

principal rafter

sole piece

SCISSOR BEAM

ARCH BRACED

SCISSOR & COLLAR

ridge piece

Common rafters

principal rafter

king post

longitudinal strut

Tie Beam

hammerbeam detail

WAGON ROOF

HAMMERBEAM ROOF

DOUBLE HAMMERBEAM

formed by a series of ribs which spring equally in all directions from a common source, and rest on a corbel. Such structures were usually put up in pairs along a roof and arranged so that the extreme ribs of each met in the centre, giving an unequalled richness to the ceiling. The point where four met was sometimes marked by a pendant, a boss or a combination of both. The spandrels between the ribs were usually treated as rectilinear panels including trefoils and quatrefoils. Perhaps the most common use for fan tracery was at the head of muntins (the vertical members) in carved screens, and more will be said of that later.

Clerestories became a standard feature and very much part of the design of the church

rather than simply an additional method of admitting natural light. They were added to many previously built churches and put up in most new ones. The designer intended them to be viewed as a whole and not as a number of individual windows. Accordingly the windows were made larger and set closer together so that they seemed to form one continuous sequence; a wall of uninterrupted glass. Where clerestories were built above the wall of an aisless nave a two-tier system of windows resulted, and the church might then have a bigger surface area of glass than masonry. The wool churches of East Anglia are particularly rich in their clerestories which have unusually large windows divided into an

98 *Needham Market Suffolk: the roof*

uncommon number of lights. Elsewhere clerestories have two or three lights beneath segmental pointed or square heads. Another feature of this period was a large window with characteristic Perpendicular tracery above the chancel arch, as if the clerestory of the nave was returned at the east end.

To say that one cannot do justice to fifteenth-century **towers** in the space here available is not simply to be defeatist. It was a period of unrivalled tower building by many local schools who between them produced a great variety of structures, generally so good that the spire became unnecessary. Where one was erected it tended to be plain, unambitious and rose like a spike from well behind the parapet. Large west windows, replacing the unbroken façade which the tower precluded, flooded the nave with light through tall tower arches. Stair turrets were standard. Some were an internal arrangement reached through a small doorway in the south interior wall. But mostly they climbed the outside of the tower, encased in an octagon which rose beside or above the parapet. Their lights were small circles, triangles or squares, in particular cusped and traceried.

In East Anglia in particular, flint and stone panelling was being lavishly used. Elsewhere towers were quite plain, while others were completely covered in panelled tracery from parapet to the strongly moulded, heavy

99 *March, Cambridgshire: the nave roof*

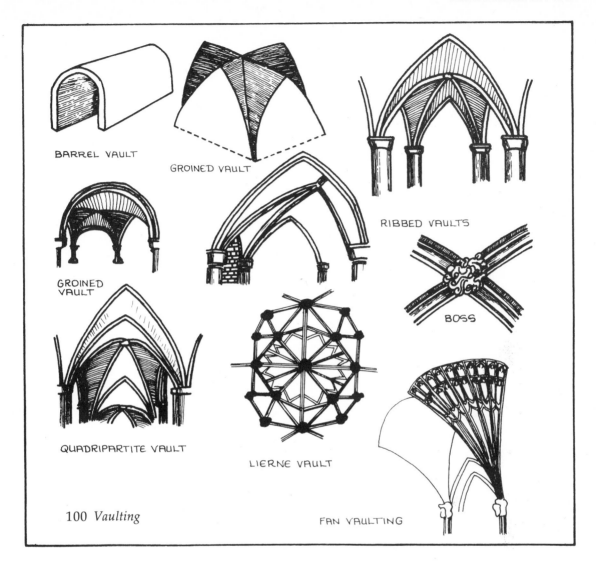

BARREL VAULT

GROINED VAULT

RIBBED VAULTS

GROINED VAULT

BOSS

QUADRIPARTITE VAULT

LIERNE VAULT

100 *Vaulting*

FAN VAULTING

plinth. Some had panelling on the lower stage, coupled or not with the belfry stage which might itself be the most richly decorated part. But by far the most common source of decoration was the parapet which in some areas had a secondary course of ornamentation immediately beneath it.

The best towers are those of Somerset, although many of the characteristics there concentrated in single structures are typical of Perpendicular work to a lesser degree elsewhere. Anything up to 12 pinnacles break the skyline; most have crockets and finials and

are carried on shafts which rest on corbels below the parapet. Some are virtually spirelets and others are of openwork carried on similar shafts.

Parapets were straight or flat, regularly battlemented or stepped. Occasionally one appears to rise in tiers. They were sometimes plain, but mostly pierced with panel work or tracery. In many instances the line of the parapet was not broken by the shafts of the pinnacles, allowing rich continuity to the top of the towers which had decorative parapets. A wide course of blind quatrefoils immediately

beneath the parapet might sometimes be repeated as a string course at the junction of the stages below. This treatment showed that the decoration of the tower was conceived as a harmonious whole, and was often borne out by the arrangement of the accompanying windows in each stage. The wall between the parapet and the belfry openings might be plain, panelled or traceried.

Belfries had two or three two-light openings, often divided by transoms and filled by masonry pierced with sound holes. The openings were usually flanked by pinnacles carried on shafts above the buttresses, or arranged as pilasters, there and between the openings. Belfry openings, when they did not extend the full width of the stage, were sometimes included within panelling or blind tracery which extended either side. Otherwise the belfry openings and the lights or panels in the stage below might be done of a piece, giving the tower a top heavy appearance.

There were sometimes two, but more often a single light in the stage below, similarly treated to the belfry opening. In four-stage towers the same pattern was usually repeated in the next stage down. Finally on the west face we come to the great window, usually above a square-headed doorway. Niches were sometimes provided over the large west window, built into the panel work or the shafts of flanking pinnacles. But there were less of them than during the preceding period.

Fifteenth-century **windows** were the epitome of the age, although there were so many of them with such similar characteristics that they became monotonous. They were made as large as possible to allow ample opportunities for the glassmaker, and given the added strength of a horizontal transom which divided the main lights and allowed both upper and lower sections to be independently treated. If the principal lights were not equally divided by the transom, the taller division was above. The windows were square-headed, semi-circular, segmental, pointed and commonly four-centred; they were never acutely pointed or ogee-shaped, although the favourite fourteenth-century curve was not lost elsewhere. The arch became depressed so that the tracery in the head was either depleted or, more usually, was carried below the springing of the arch.

Stone mullions ran vertically from sill to head, forming the main divisions and the limits of the individual lights which were sub-divided into two above by thinner tracery bars. The result is known as rectilinear tracery; a series of cusped panels.

The flowing forms of Decorated tracery posed problems for both the glassmakers who were required to fit their glass into the strangest shapes, and the glass painter. Prior to the fifteenth century the latter rarely treated his window as a single theme since the shape of the tracery meant that small figures, etc. had to be put into awkward shapes. Schools of glass painting were set up in many areas.

Once mullions were carried straight into the head, the painter was able to see the window as a whole and decorated it accordingly. The composition of rectilinear windows meant that he could use the divisions in the head as panels or niches. Although there was not an abundance of painted or stained glass, the masons clearly designed their windows to accommodate the glass painter and this was the golden age of the latter. Large overall pictures were produced. They included buildings and landscapes as well as biblical figures in tableau. Small windows as well as the individual sections of larger ones were filled with angels, saints and heraldic devices. The colour in the rest of the church complemented but could not match the beauty of the glass, and it is a great pity that but for a handful of complete windows only fragments remain, often collected together from several sources. When unpainted, the thin transluscent glass of the fifteenth century let in a silvery light.

There was more **colour** in the fifteenth-century church than at any other time. Nothing was whitewashed. The walls were full of murals; capitals were painted. Light

◄101 *Cullompton, Devon: the south chapel*

103 *Taunton, Somerset: exceptionally high, detailed and perfect tower*

102 *Cricklade, Wiltshire: heavy crossing tower decorated inside and out*

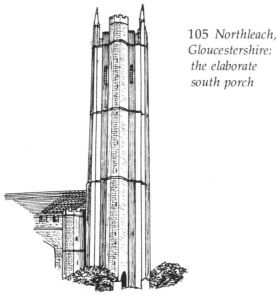

105 *Northleach, Gloucestershire: the elaborate south porch*

104 *Ashburton, Devon: impressive west tower of grey stone*

82

from the new clerestories poured onto doom paintings above the chancel arch: awful reminders of the Day of Judgement put up, perhaps, as the thank offering of a traveller come safely home. Wooden chancel and parclose screen were coloured, as were the timber roofs.

The size of **porches,** particularly those belonging to larger churches, increased in both area and height. The proportions improved and some, especially those with an upper room, were built on a vertical double-cube plan. This room was used as a library, archives store, schoolroom, courthouse, or as the quarters of the sacristan

106 *Cirencester, Gloucestershire: the south porch, built late in the fifteenth century*

with especial interest in the safe keeping of the church plate. Many included one or two windows divided into lights with rectilinear tracery, and in some cases even transoms of size which would not disgrace the clerestory. They were always put into the front wall of the porch, the side walls of the upper room being usually left unpierced. Some porches, which were simply tall but had no room above, included large side windows with sills on the base moulding of the porch, but traceried heads well above the height of the door.

A number of north and south porches were put up at around the same time in wealthy areas, and it is wrong to suppose that a south porch was automatically the first choice. In many places the position of the church in relation to the village determined which was the first entrance to be built, which was the main one and which was the most highly decorated. Otherwise – and this was usually true where the south porch was the main one yet less decorated than the north, or where the latter was a later addition – a wealthy merchant or landowner might be responsible.

Given a greater surface area, what was more natural than to decorate it? The two stages were often separated by a string course which might be deep and richly ornamented. Less ambitious examples have a typical square label above the finely proportioned arch mouldings of the doorway. With panel-work prevalent in window tracery, the porch and any buttresses were usually treated as a series of panels cusped, quatrefoiled and including reticulated tracery. Heraldic shields over the doorway often indicate who was responsible for the structure. Even the simplest porches, put up in small village churches, were rarely without niches. There might be three or more in larger buildings, stooled, canopied and treated as part of a series of panels across the front of the porch. Spandrels and the spaces between the elements of tracery were liberally treated to multifoils, figurework, vines, foliage and diaper patterns. Special mention must here be made of the beautiful East Anglian stone and flint panelling, known as flushwork, often used in conjunction with tracery, stone niches and accessories.

Varied decoration continued to the very point at which the line of the porch met the sky, often flanked by pinnacles raised above the cornice or as a continuation of the buttresses. The porch might be gabled to a greater or lesser degree or might have a simply embattled parapet, stepped battlements or a parapet of openwork which was either battlemented or took the line of the particular decoration. Most of the smaller porches had open-type wooden roofs, perhaps with a tie-beam and occasionally a collar, arch brace or king post. Fine fan vaulting occurs in large ones.

Like all arches **doorways** were wider and flatter, with commonly a segmental pointed arch on the inside. Some were deeply recessed with slender shafts and plainly moulded caps in the jambs. Many had ogee-shaped dripstones beneath a pointed or square-headed hood moulding, or else the moulding ran over a four-centred arch. The spandrels were richly decorated with rectilinear tracery, panelling, cusped circles, quatrefoils, coats of arms or foliage.

A great change came over the ornamentation of **doors.** The profusion of metal scrollwork gave way to the delicate forms of intricate tracery, confining the art of the smith to hinges, latches and handles. The woodcarver saw the door as a blind window, carving mullions below, curvilinear or rectilinear tracery in the head. Sometimes the spaces between the mullions included vertical floral and figure work.

The great period of rebuilding meant that many new arcades were put up. The pier caps came closer to the crown of the arch as the latter tended to flatten, visually enhancing the height of the piers. As the period advanced arches became more obtuse and the four-centred or Tudor arch which made its appearance in the middle of the century had by c. 1485 achieved considerable popularity for doors and windows as well as in arcades. Some arches were straight-sided and heads

might also be round, segmental or flat. Mouldings were wide and shallow and sometimes continued unbroken around the arch and down to the floor. In such instances the sub-arch might be decorated by a band of quatrefoil panelling.

Piers were tall and slender. In the larger churches the fourteenth-century style of clustered columns continued to be popular, as did groups of four, eight or more engaged columns set against a larger central core. Village churches had either clusters of four columns, which were lozenge-shaped in plan, plain circular or octagonal shaped piers. In the clusters thick and thin shafts alternated with a wide variety of shallow concave mouldings between. The arch mouldings above a composite pier were frequently a continuation of the shafts carried individually above independent caps. Until the fifteenth century the arrangement between the shaft and the arch was always clearly defined. Now the abacus, bell and astragal were merged together. Perpendicular masons were undecided on the result and provided no one style for the period.

Perpendicular caps were generally narrower and taller than their predecessors. They were altogether omitted when the mouldings of the piers were continued right around the head of the arch, with no moulded indication of the point of springing. Sometimes a tiny cap was set in position on only the inner moulding. Otherwise the abacus was of little importance and although the upper moulding of the cap was sometimes a roll or still the decorated ogee shape, the vast majority began with a straight slope, the chamfer developing into a rounded edge or square fillet with an ogee quarter round beneath.

The shape of the capital might be circular or octagonal over a shaft or shafts of either kind. Otherwise the mouldings might be continuous around a group of caps set over a composite pier. The bell of the circular type was often shallow and plain, whereas the surfaces of octagonal caps leant themselves to a variety of motifs and themes. Most of the carvings were done shallowly and little foliage was attempted. Occasionally large leaves wrapped themselves around the bells but carving was often, if not exactly stiff in the Early English sense of the word, certainly restrained. Angels came out of the roofs and attached themselves to the surface of the caps, invariably holding shields. There were other heraldic devices, instruments of the passion and everyday life, and some figure sculpture. Occasionally caps were battlemented, and when some form of this was applied to an octagonal shape with a row of four-leaved flowers below, the appearance was that of a crown.

Bases took on an unprecedented importance and were considerably increased in height. Even in relatively small country churches this allowed for a two-tier base construction, with each element of a different design. Where the pier above included several shafts, each often had its own independent base, although a group was usually treated as a whole as regards mouldings; because the whole structure was so much more slender the upper base appeared to be even further from the floor. This considerably aided experiments in proportion which had succeeded the obsession with light and shade all over the church. It was also another area in which masons were working with the juxtaposition of octagonal and circular shapes. The roll moulding was more pronounced on the base and the double ogee survived, often developing into a quirk.

Plinths hardly projected from the line of the lower base which they closely followed in plan.

Except in Cornwall where earlier designs prevailed and infrequently elsewhere where there were sophisticated tubs, fifteenth-century **fonts** had octagonal bowls on similar pedestals. We find not only local types of general design, but also of artistic concept and execution. Many of them were originally coloured and might still be so but for the indifferent ways in which the intervening

layers of whitewash were removed. Generally, what distinguishes a Perpendicular font is the way in which each surface of the bowl and stem is treated as an individual panel, and the extent to which the underside of the bowl is similarly ornamented. The carvers seemed unable to let go of an idea once it had occurred to them, and the result was a monotonous plethora of intricately done, solemn figurework. So much had not been seen since the Normans, but its intention was to instruct and there is nothing in it of spontaneity or entertainment. The only criteria seemed to be the amount of money which could be raised for the project, and on that was determined the extent and quality of the sculpture.

The panels of the bowl were frequently recessed and separated by buttresses with pinnacles. The scenes were sculpted under finialed canopies which often had rectilinear tracery in the spandrels. Each face was treated independently with a biblical scene or a moment from the life of a saint or martyr, and the figurework was nicely proportioned. The faces of less sophisticated bowls were filled with one or two figures; otherwise heraldic or blank shields, instruments of the Passion, Tudor roses, symbols of the evangelists, cinquefoiled lights or angels – sometimes variously combined. Angels, too, were a favourite theme for the underside of the bowl where, like the leaves of flowers which were similarly placed, their outspread wings either touched or overlapped. The underside of the bowls approached the stem with a variety of devices. They might be corbelled out on the backs of angels, variously moulded or decorated, or the transition might be effected by a band of floral decoration.

The stem was also commonly panelled with buttresses between; simple blind tracery in the poorer ones, otherwise canopied single figures. In some cases the figures or animals were free standing on pedestals. Bases and plinths were also octagonal, the former either plainly moulded or including a band of minor decoration. Tall plinths were usually decorated on each face by double or triple panels of pierced or traceried quatrefoils, sometimes set diagonally or encircled and cusped.

Special mention must be made of the East Anglian seven sacraments fonts. These are octagonal and characteristically treated, except that the panels depict the sacraments in variable sequence leaving the eighth side to be filled by a suitable moment from the scriptures. In particular these fonts were sometimes raised above a sequence of steps, in some cases taking the form of a Maltese Cross.

In the far west of the country wooden **screens** often form the only division between nave and chancel, and extend the full width of the church. A chancel screen becomes a rood screen when it incorporates the cross and crucifix. In many places it replaced the chancel arch and completely eclipsed it in others, for it became the most lavishly and richly carved furnishing, gilded or brightly coloured. Some were of stone.

Most screens are divided into a number of similar bays pierced and traceried with lights above and a corresponding number of plain or blind traceried panels below. In the centre is either a wider opening or one similarly treated to the bays, but forming double doors. Other doors, usually no wider than the width of each bay, may occur if the screen crosses aisles. The best examples are in Devonshire. They have an elaborate cornice, topped by cresting and including several horizontal bands of intricate decoration of vines, tendrils and almost any of the motifs of the day. The arched heads beneath are filled with fan vaulting with moulded ribs, traceried panels and bosses.

Elsewhere there was a moulded top rail between the lower band of the cornice and the heads of the lights. Most screens had a deep plinth, separated from the lower panels by a horizontal rail. These panels frequently included painted figures. Whilst the screens of the West Country tended to be lavishly ornamented but squat with thick styles and muntins, elsewhere the openings were taller and the screens generally higher with little by way of a cornice. Sometimes there was no more than an upper rail, surmounted by brattishing. **Parclose screens** which divided chantry chapels from the nave were similarly designed but rarely as highly decorated.

On top of the rood screen was a **rood loft** reached by a stairway which ran through the wall on the north side and emerged onto the loft, some way above the ground. Many of these openings, especially those which opened onto the loft, still exist. Rood lofts were used by the choir and musicians. They had high panelled fronts, often with the great rood and the flanking figures of the Virgin Mary and St John the Evangelist built into them. If this was not the case, the rood was fixed to a heavy beam above. Like the screen, the rood loft often had a cornice of several decorated bands below an elaborate cresting.

6
Renaissance and Classical 1547-1830

NEARLY two and three-quarter centuries of classical architecture in England spanned eleven reigns, the Reformation, the Commonwealth, the Restoration of the Monarchy, physical desecration of church property and sweeping changes in liturgy. Elizabethan and Jacobean (1558–1625) are the periods of the Early Renaissance when changes began to appear firstly in the design and decoration of monuments and thence progressed to other fixtures and fittings. Then (1625–1830) came the Late Renaissance of Stuart and Georgian architecture, including the Classical Age which began at the restoration of 1660. It was so called because from then until about the middle of the eighteenth century a succession of architects, inspired by Italian, French and Flemish recreations of the architecture of Imperial Rome, attempted to revive it structurally and decoratively in both church and secular building. The classical period applied to church art and architecture can be subdivided into the three main influences. These were the Age of Wren (1669–1721), and the two which occurred during the Georgian era – the Baroque (1700–1750), and Palladian (from 1750).

The architecture of Imperial Rome was more elaborate than that of Ancient Greece and it employed the constructional arch which was unknown to the Greeks. Otherwise it was based on Doric, Ionic and Corinthian, the names the Romans gave to the three Classical Orders of Ancient Greece. They added two of

their own: Tuscan and Composite. The whole field of Roman architecture was exemplified in *De Architectura*, a treatise by the first-century architect and writer Vitruvius. It was Palladio's study of Vitruvius' writings, resulting in his own work and that of his followers, which inspired Inigo Jones to his particular variation on the Italian Renaissance style. The style which reached England was already hybrid, yet it developed into a native renaissance.

A Classical Order consists of an entablature and the kind of pillar which supports it, both of which have particular characteristics. The former is the arrangement of horizontal bands and mouldings of – in ascending order – architrave, frieze and cornice. These features are not necessarily confined to load-bearing pillars and may appear in whole or part around the upper section of interior walls. The pillar comprises capital, shaft and base; there may be an abacus between the capital and architrave, and an astragal between the bell and shaft.

Roman **Doric** was fairly plain, although the tapered shaft might be fluted and the frieze above could include vertically-grooved blocks known as triglyphs. Rectangular projections called dentils were often present in the capital or cornice. The **Ionic** shaft was slender and fluted, the capital being distinguished by the volute or spiral scroll at each corner. It was not uncommon for figure work to feature in the frieze. The **Corinthian** shaft was usually plain, but the capital had a mass of spiky leaves:

laurel, olive or acanthus piled one on top of the other, spreading upwards and outwards. **Tuscan** was a mixture of Doric and Composite; it consisted of plain mouldings at either end of a plain shaft, an arrangement which became extremely popular in English Renaissance architecture. **Composite** was a mixture of Ionic and Corinthian, taking large volutes on its capital from the former. Its shaft was fluted. Projecting rectangular brackets called mutules occasionally decorated a frieze or architrave and the small square drops which seem to hang below are known as guttae. The spaces between triglyphs are called metopes, and they sometimes include figurework.

Bases were created of simple concave and convex mouldings in varying depths. The occasional fillet might be inserted, invariably above a convex moulding. The customary 'Attic base' to an Ionic pillar, for example, consisted of a concave scotia hollow between two large convex tori. Another arrangement was two narrow astragals with a scotia hollow above and a large torus below. Both the Doric and Tuscan bases commonly comprised a fillet or shallow astragal above a torus. The more elaborate pillars might have a pair of astragals beneath a hollow, resting on a large torus. Plinths were uniformly square.

Classical **ornamentation** was bold and deeply cut. It included fruit and foliage, birds, cherubs, shells and masks. The former were both stylised and naturalistic, but lusciously portrayed; the rest looked healthy and well fed. Most easily recognisable is the rather spiky upright acanthus leaf which adorns Corinthian capitals, and cornices and friezes where it took over from brattishing. The anthemion or honeysuckle, bay leaf and lily are also commonly depicted; foliage and fruit combined in short horizontal trails are known as festoons. When worked up to enclose panels, they are known as wreaths or garlands. Loosely folded material was similarly treated; on its own it might be a ribband or otherwise looped as if caught on pegs to form a swag. There were several variations of the scroll and an amount of

interlacing; so too the Greek key, fret or lattice. An interlaced banding of Flemish origin, called strapwork, became popular. Amongst the smaller motifs the bead went ever on and, when alternated with a small diamond and fillet device, was known as bead and reel. An elongated bead alternating with a downward pointing arrow is egg and dart, becoming egg and tongue where the oval is raised above a lip. The guilloche was the result of two loosely plaited strands running horizontally and often enclosing a small flower.

The Florentine sculptor Pietro Torrigiani completed Henry VII's fine tomb in Westminister Abbey in 1519. English Gothic was at its height, but Torrigiani's work was full Italian Renaissance. Fine Tudor churches were being built in the Perpendicular style which was to linger until the Commonwealth and, after a brief period of architectural inactivity, even beyond the Restoration of the Monarchy. Some classical detail appeared in a few minor pieces during the next few years but its constructional possibilities were not to be quickly realised in English Church architecture. In 1534 Henry VIII assumed control of the Church of England by an Act of Supremacy, so eclipsing the inspiration behind the great Perpendicular buildings. Interest shifted to domestic architecture and the religious fire went out.

At the beginning of the Reformation in England the country was staunchly Catholic and the reformers were comparatively few. Massive amounts of money had recently been spent on the country's churches. Internally the Church was divided and some bishops favoured a suppression of monastic powers. People were not disillusioned with the teaching of Rome but with the teachers. The monasteries had become rich landowners, greedy and covetous. The clergy were lazy, claiming all the material benefits they could but giving little in return. Reform was inevitable even if Henry VIII's private quarrel proved to be the timely catalyst.

Henry followed up the seizure of the Church with a number of statutes such as the Act for the Submission of the Clergy. This isolated them from any appeals to Rome and effectively gave him control of all religious matters. Thomas Cromwell made a comprehensive inventory – *Valor Ecclesiasticus* – of the Church's wealth in lands, buildings and valuables. In 1536 some 370 of the smaller foundations were dissolved by Act of Parliament to pay for secular expenditure, and the next four years saw the wholesale appropriation of the larger houses: the Dissolution of the Monasteries.

Attention then swung to the parish churches. Royal arms began to be put up (made compulsory after 1660) and bells were silenced or pulled down. Church building stopped, only to be renewed very slowly after the accession of Elizabeth I. Revolutionary groups were working from within the established Church, aiming variously to destroy either elements in its worship and doctrine or, amongst the more militant, all Anglicanism as they knew it. These people were known as Puritans from the early 1570s. The prelude to their atrocities had been Nicholas Ridley's move to replace stone altars with Communion tables which went into the nave where they could be surrounded on three sides by the congregation. Nearly a century later William Laud was to give his name to a style of rail, when he urged that such tables should be railed off at the east end like altars.

Cranmer and his associates introduced the First Book of Common Prayer in 1549. It was compiled from Catholic and Protestant sources, and was amended by both Parliament and the Clergy. Emphasis shifted to the sermon as the essence of the service, and in gradually bringing together the Minister and the congregation effectively altered the working shape of the mediaeval church. Side chapels were unnecessary, a fact that assisted the destruction to come. When the centralised congregation expanded, it did so sideways so that the length of the nave was no longer a particular feature and the width increased.

Edwards VI's commissioners heralded a Puritan onslaught aimed at doing away with anything 'superstitious'. Down came the great rood which was in every church, together with the flanking carvings of the Virgin Mary and St John. Rood lofts were removed in their entirety. Effigies and carvings from both inside the church and without were either mutilated, smashed up or burnt. The great wealth of mediaeval painted glass disappeared into fragments; wall paintings went under plaster and whitewash. Fonts were taken outside and either broken up or put to secular use. Even the carvings in many roofs were removed.

This destruction lasted for a quarter of a century and left the churches of England stripped of their colour, art and workmanship, which had taken centuries to evolve. It stopped at the succession of Mary Tudor, who had always wanted to re-establish links with Rome but had been persuaded of the wisdom of a political compromise. She continued to celebrate the Catholic Mass, although theoretically forbidden to do so under the Act of Uniformity of 1549. In most churches both the service and surroundings were very different.

Elizabeth also compromised. During her reign most work in the church was confined to fittings and there was little actual building. The Puritans were present but restrained, under a more liberal interpretation of Henry VIII and Edward VI's views of Protestantism – ignoring Mary's brief return to the Church of Rome. Elizabeth decreed that the Commandments should be displayed at the East end; other biblical texts were written on the walls and bells again rang across the countryside. Under her Act of Uniformity (1559) the situation was rationalised and the Church declared Reformed. In the churches of the land there was much to be done by way of repair and restoration, but so much irreplaceable material had been destroyed for ever.

The reign of James I at least achieved a measure of co-operation between Anglican and Puritan in the publication in 1611 of the Authorized version of the Bible. Otherwise a few plain, solid churches were built in a mixture of Gothic and Renaissance styles and only a handful are known to have been built during the first half of the seventeenth century. The latter style was strangely done, for those who practised it gleaned their interest of Roman architecture from pictures. Mostly it was applied to monuments. In 1638 Inigo Jones laid the foundation stone of St Paul's, Covent Garden and in so doing became the first English architect to construct a whole building in the Classical style. He had travelled extensively in Italy, being greatly influenced by the work of Andrea Palladio. It is sad that although Inigo Jones designed the first structurally Renaissance church in England and was the best exponent of the Palladian style, his work was curtailed by his Royalist allegiance.

At length the smouldering Puritans burst out in violent opposition to the Church and the Anglican monarch Charles I. He was supported by Archbishop Laud who had restored the altar to the east end, set up a reredos behind it and railed it off to keep out dogs and provide a point for the congregation to receive Communion. Laud declared the English Church a part of the Catholic Church, defended its liturgy and the unchanged nature of its being. Before the restoration of prayer book and monarchy, before the Puritans were to splinter into Presbyterians and Congregationalists, came civil war and ten years of the Commonwealth. Churches were brutally misused, their fixtures and fittings were destroyed with wanton vandalism, and those who attended them in hope of the Restoration were poorly compensated by the words of their incumbents.

The fire which burned London began on 2 September 1666. In its wake were the ruins of 87 churches. The decision to build 53 on their former sites cramped within the mediaeval lanes of the city, and entrust the work to the barely tried Sir Christopher Wren, gave

impetus to Wren's interpretation of the new style. It provided an unexpected foothold carved out of necessity. Outside the capital the churches were more than equal to the demands made on them. Ravaged from several quarters and deprived of much visual splendour, they were no longer at the centre of community life, and there was little to be said for many who preached in them. Consequently there are few village churches of the Wren period and hardly any which resemble those of London. Occasionally a country church was built to the mediaeval plan and internal arrangement, but in the Renaissance style: an arcade of Classical pillars and round arches divided by a cornice from the clerestory above. From now on the work was in the hands of named architects and craftsmen; professionals who paved the way for a great tide of gifted amateurs in the provinces.

Wren never studied the Italian Renaissance at source, although he met Gianlorenzo Bernini who was in Paris at the invitation of Louis XIV, but was influenced by its exponents. Steeped in Gothic tradition but with little love for it, he occasionally built in the late Perpendicular style. This is shown in the proportions of his steeples and the way in which, where space allowed, he built on the traditional nave and flanking aisles plan. But **Wren's London Churches** are very much the result of compromise and in some cases success over the several problems with which he had to contend. The change in liturgy to the central preaching requirement of Protestant worship made him more conscious of the ways in which his designs could fundamentally fulfil the purpose of the building. He had the size of the congregation to consider and the varying amounts of money available for each project. There were the sites, and the overall effect of so many churches in such close proximity to each other and so many other buildings. Visually, there was little point in great overall enrichment, and Wren realised that the limits of space imposed on him meant that the main interest

107 *St Stephen's, Walbrook, City of London (1672–7) by Christopher Wren*▶

109 *Willen, Buckinghamshire (1679–80) by Robert Hooke*

108 *Ingestre, Staffordshire (1676) by Christopher Wren*

110 *Farley, Wiltshire, built by 1689–90*

111 *Frampton, Dorset (1695)*

would be concentrated on the street elevation and skyline.

In plan these London churches were traditional rectangles, with one or two aisles, internally arranged as a Greek Cross, square, oval, or rough approximations of these shapes. They might have vaults or domes. It is interesting that Wren had to cope with so many constraints which were unknown to previous architects and builders. He had to divide his time between the individual

craftsmen who were working within his basic concept of utilitarianism, and much of the work considered characteristic of a Wren church was that of the finest craftsmen of the day.

The skyline was changed by **towers and spires** which combined Gothic and Renaissance features; steeples done in lead and stone. They rise in stages, with curving sides, cupolas and domes. There are square and round colonnades, diagonal columns, balustrades, obelisks and urns. Each stage was individually treated, many taking the form of an opening flanked by freestanding or engaged Classical pillars with or without a pediment. This arrangement is known as an aedicule and in many cases the spires of Wren churches are a diminishing succession of aedicules ending in an obelisk or spirelet with finial.

Internally, the churches were single rectangular chambers. Classical pillars on high pedestals supported ceilings of rich plaster-work above a decorated entablature. Altars were given particular importance, enhanced by carved and painted altar pieces. High backed pews were arranged to command fine views of the rich pulpit with its decorated sounding board. Large windows, full of clear glass, flooded the interior with light.

In 1711 Parliament passed an Act for building 50 new churches. Although only 12 were built before interest waned it gave opportunity to exponents of the Baroque, a free and exuberant neo-Classical style which enjoyed considerable popularity in England during the first half of the eighteenth century. Most were designed by or with the help of Wren's pupil Nicholas Hawksmoor, who also worked for Sir John Vanbrugh. His churches were at once original and solidly overpowering. Other disciples of the style who designed churches in London and the provinces over the next few years included Thomas Archer, who was a pupil of Vanbrugh, James Gibbs, who studied in Italy, and John James. George Dance the Elder also built in the Classical style. None of these architects possessed Wren's genius, but they were amongst the last to share a common desire to build to the glory of God. Their buildings had imposing façades to the street, and were large and externally grand. Churches were soon to pass through a comfortable drawing room stage and to emerge as little more than halls.

The Classical Age was also known as the Pillar and Portico era. A **portico** is a roofed area, supported by an arrangement of columns and open on at least one side. Its upper frontage takes the form of a **pediment,** a low-pitched, ornamental gable. Most were enclosed within a cornice which ran horizontally at the base but followed the chosen shape of the pediment above. Where the cornices were unbroken and not in themselves of a particularly ornate nature, such as the most common triangular type, they formed tympanums which might be left blank or enriched with escutcheons, garlands or figure and classical sculpture in relief. Some contained a circular window. A broken pediment occurred when the cornice did not run across the entire width at its base but finished as projections returned inwards above a pillar on either side. The segmental pediment was shaped like a quarter of a circle rising above the cornice of the entablature, and where the quarter round is not completed the pediment is said to be open. An open pediment with a cornice ending in whorls is said to be scrolled, and the swan-necked type

112 *Portland, Dorset (1754–66) by Thomas Gilbert*

are given graceful, flowing curves to their sides which end almost in finials which resemble the bird's head.

Together, the arrangement of portico and pediment was erected as the frontage to the main entrance of many classical churches designed by Wren, his followers and successors. But the pediment is to be found elsewhere; as the gable on relatively small porches, in village churches, above doorways and windows, wall monuments and memorials. In many instances of the latter, broken or open types were often used to admit large coats of arms which frequently exceeded the height of the tympanum. External pediments and those associated with larger monuments sometimes have a characteristic urn or obelisk at the apex and elsewhere.

The symbol of the early Renaissance in England was the turned **baluster** which helped support a rail and when put up in sequence was known as a balustrade. Introduced late in the sixteenth century, this vertical, bulbous colonnette was invariably fatter in either its middle or base. Externally, it featured as parapets and window dressings. Internally it appeared on 'Laudian' communion rails which enclosed the altar, general altar rails and galleries.

What happened in village churches was more a question of shifting furniture around within the old **plan.** At the suppression of gilds and chantries several altars disappeared from various aisles and transepts, and only piscinas remain – or perhaps parts of a reredos – to indicate where they were. Altars came into the nave which, together with extra space afforded by the transepts, was treated as all round accommodation for the congregation. Many arcades were rebuilt during the seventeenth century using Classical, especially Tuscan, columns and high round arches. When the altar was reinstated at the east end, it was sometimes given an apse and its importance enhanced by a reredos.

The **auditory plan** of the seventeenth century allowed everyone taking part in the

113 *Hardenhuish, Wiltshire (1779) by John Wood*

service to be accommodated in a single undivided interior. It became more important to increase the width of the building rather than its length so that people could be nearer the preacher when he delivered his sermon. Where congregations were large the overflow from the floor could be accommodated by a gallery around three sides of the room, supported by classical pillars.

In the villages the squire sometimes rebuilt parts of the mediaeval church, adding galleries and furnishing his own sumptuous family pew. Otherwise he might, especially after the Reformation and influenced by the work of Wren and his followers, build a similarly styled church to his own country house. The eighteenth century was the time of the amateur architect, but from the Restoration architects and artists were named; they were pupils and followers of one another.

Three-quarters of the way through the eighteenth century we still have a few country churches being put up in what can be called Georgian Gothic. They might combine tracery, arches, parapet and pinnacles of Decorated inspiration set in external **walls** which are essentially eighteenth-century; plain and without strings. To some extent the place of the latter had been taken by the **cornice** where it encompassed a steeple as it continued on its horizontal plane beneath the roof of the church, superseding the corbel table. Stone walls were constructed with ashlar blocks which were large and regular. The corners were sometimes made to look stronger by being formed as a pillar of rectangular blocks placed one on top of the other. These might be capped by characteristic urns set on plinths, rising above the cornice and flanking the gables at the west and east ends. Some churches were built entirely of pink brick; others had stone quoins or else the corners of the building were of alternating brick and stone. Stone banding and accessories

contrasted with the brickwork. Carved panels or swags of fruit and foliage were sometimes put up over windows. The west end of the building which could not hitherto be designed as a façade because a tower was in the way, might now have a portico with the steeple rising above and in no way interfering with the arrangement of columns and pediment. By the early eighteenth century the elevation of many churches resembled that of domestic architecture, an upper row of windows allowing light into the galleries. The gable, hitherto the usual feature of east and west ends, was occasionally put up in the form of a pediment over the south door – itself moved to a central position. Small, towerless churches had caps or domes rising above open arches with cornice, all of which stood on a square base.

Plain parapets or balstrades hid lead gutters and low pitched **roofs.** The eaves were supported by a moulded cornice which might be formed into pediments at the gable ends and sometimes over the main doorway if it was in another wall.

By the seventeenth century fashionable ceilings were of moulded plasterwork. Ribbands, swags, luscious fruit and foliage, patera and healthy cherubs adorned soffits and

114 *Blandford, Dorset (1733–9) by John and William Bastard*

115 *Gayhurst, Buckinghamsire (1728)*

panels everywhere including spandrels – all done up in sumptuous wreaths. An arrangement of sunk and decorated ceiling panels of varying sizes is said to be coffered; otherwise panels might contain paintings. Some ceilings were a rich overall decoration of linked, smaller motifs in relief. Painting was done in white, gold and pastel shades. General designs and individual motifs were of a secular nature, originating in the big houses and transferred to the church. At its most ornate, a riot of gold and white plasterwork, flamboyant and gilded stucco was the Rococo successor to Baroque.

Few Renaissance churches had **buttresses;** they were of brick and otherwise featureless. Yet the flat **pilaster** survived and now, with Classical cap and base, continued to give vertical punctuation to both external and interior walls. It became a feature of internal east and west walls, marking the extent of bays, often flanking windows and in line with the free-standing pillars where there would once have been the responds of the nave arcades.

Gone were the soaring Gothic **towers** whose inspiration must have seemed as strange to the eighteenth-century churchgoer as did most mediaeval decoration, and it was not until the end of the century that many attempts were made to understand it. Renaissance towers were plain and unbuttressed: low, sturdy and square in plan. Even the lower stages of Wren's church towers were plain, although there might be considerable Classical decoration above. The more ambitious country church might have a small lantern or modest cupola surmounting its tower. Nowhere was there a **steeple** to rival those of the later seventeenth- and early eighteenth-century London churches, although one or two were put up latterly in larger provincial towns. Some were examples of strangely stylised Gothic, with broaches and the occasional flying buttress.

Parapets too were plain, or otherwise openwork Classical balustrades with an urn or obelisk at each angle. Sometimes these rested on stone plinths of the same depth as the parapet, and stone was also used as dressing, around windows and as banding if the tower was divided into stages. Where they were made of brick, quoins or cornerstones might also be of stone and the latter were sometimes rusticated so that they appeared to provide the extra stability previously associated with buttresses. They normally ascended the full height of the tower to the cornice. Windows were either square-headed or round-headed,

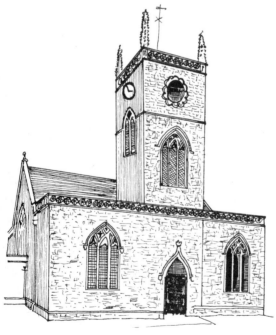

116 *Moreton, Dorset (1776) by James Frampton*

117 *Glynde, Sussex (1765)*

96

often inserted in only the belfry stage. Occasionally a round window was inserted below.

Fairly large **windows** which were not divided by flat mullions or transoms commonly had semi-circular heads. Otherwise they were depressed or flat-headed. The points of spring might be marked by rectangular impost blocks, occasionally forming shoulders to the flatter arch. An exaggerated keystone protruded at the crown. There was little cusping done after the middle of the seventeenth century. Although Wren's churches sometimes contained stained glass and a small amount of glass painting was done in the eighteenth century, windows of the period were usually filled with small leaded, rectangular panes. A round-headed window flanked by square ones was known as a Venetian window. Wholly semi-circular lights are called lunettes.

Gone now, as a general rule, was the large east window. Its place was taken by high altar pieces with their panels of paintings and texts, or the equally conspicuous carved reredos. Some round-headed windows were put up behind the altar where they were partly obscured by these features or, if there was some space above, a lunette might be inserted. Such commonly formed a clerestory, whilst the larger round-headed windows flanked the altar piece and were put up in the side walls. Oval windows were extremely popular in both clerestory and lower stages. They often filled the heads of arches when viewed from the inside, and were similarly put up for effect where they encompassed wall features.

Porches were not common. In larger town churches they were succeeded by the Classical portico; an arrangement of between four and six columns across the face of the building, with two or three columns at right angles on either side. Otherwise porches were semi-circular in plan with six or more columns supporting either a flat or domed roof. The

118 *St Martin's in the Fields, London (1721–6) by James Gibbs*

entablature would here be curved and there would be no pediment above, as would also be the case when the entablature was surmounted by a balustrade.

Renaissance motifs began to appear around **doorways** early in the seventeenth century when an entablature occasionally surmounted a Gothic arch. Classical doorways had round arches, sometimes springing from moulded abaci and composed of large, sometimes oddly shaped voussoirs. Keystones might be projecting or exaggerated. The openings were flanked by flat, set-back pilasters with Classical caps and bases, or scrolled brackets known as consoles. Pediments above sometimes had recessed tympanums.

Arches of the Classical Age were semi-circular, elliptical and high. Combined with the types of pillars described elsewhere they allowed maximum light to be used as efficiently and effectively as possible. Ordered arches disappeared with Perpendicular Gothic and they now had flat soffits or undersides. A prominent keystone or panel was sometimes carved. In the country traditional nave arcades were occasionally built in the Classical style, but the arches in larger town churches might be constructed as barrel vaults across the bays of the aisles where they continued the decorated entablature.

Even greater than the change in the architecture of **monuments and tombs** was that of the whole approach to the subject. In less than 100 years the mediaeval thought behind the pious effigy, flat on its back and reverently craving admittance into the hereafter in prayer, had gone. Figures with a tendency towards mediaevalism were recumbent but more natural in expression and detail with their eyes closed. The effigy was inclined, its hands resting apart either across the body or at its side. Fairly early in the sixteenth century figures began to kneel; a similar pose being later adopted by weepers as well as other members of the deceased's family, particularly children. Even family pets appeared. The decline in religious thought

gradually gave more importance to the deceased than his predicament. Not only were secular poses prominent, they were forcibly portrayed as if the subjects were in many instances commanding their place in Heaven. They stood, surrounded by the tools of their trades or symbols of their calling, either actively engaged or standing, staring back across the church. From the late seventeenth century the subjects were commonly dressed in Roman clothes which later became Classical draperies of an unspecified type. In the eighteenth century the subjects were heavily bewigged and adopted semi-recumbent postures, beautifully dressed but either lolling about or shown in almost theatrical poses.

The move away from chantry chapels meant that whilst these were becoming family pews, huge monuments and tombs were being erected to commemorate the deceased and immediate relations. These occupied considerable floor or wall space and, like the poses of the figures, were full of variety. Heraldry – the crests and shields of family alliances – added considerably to the colour in tombs and monuments which lingered through the sixteenth and seventeenth centuries and only stopped during the eighteenth. A single overpowering tomb or wall monument built against the chancel or aisle wall often completely dominates what are otherwise small and unprepossessing country churches. They may include likenesses, medallions or busts of both the deceased and other members of the family.

The English Renaissance first showed itself in Flemish and Italian inspired monuments in country churches. They were done in native and imported stones, coloured marbles or alabaster. With the eighteenth century came a preference for black and white and pure white marbles. The latter produced some startling effects, particularly where death was represented by a skeleton or the upper half of the deceased emerged from a recess or urn. Great attention was paid to clothing, draperies and soft furnishings, making the effigies as comfortable in death as they were in their own drawing rooms which, latterly, were being represented in the furnishings of the church.

Tombs and monuments had moulded canopies supported by Classical pillars of all Orders, surmounted by obelisks. Chubby winged angels or medallions adorned canopies. Wall monuments in particular were topped by variously styled pediments. Free-standing urns were common, placed on Classical bases, either of which might be inscribed. Classically draped angels, cherubs and damsels were used structurally, decoratively and symbolically. As caryatids they were used as pillars, or in other supporting roles such as corbels or brackets. Ribbands, garlands and characteristic strapwork appeared both as cresting and minor decoration.

The other great change associated with monuments was in the type of inscription. The art of lettering was at its most excellent, compelled to expound a lengthy catalogue of the deceased's virtues in this life – a set of references to accompany him into the next. More conservative inscriptions abounded in **wall memorials** and **cartouches.** The latter were tablets, often elaborately framed, in the form of an open scroll. Wall memorials might be simply done; arms in a roundel above the inscription – or more commonly consisted of arms in a pediment, supported by Classical pillars flanking the inscription, resting on a shelf with brackets beneath. Otherwise memorial tablets simply recorded the barest details of the deceased and might be of almost any shape. Many of these items are remarkable for the panels of sculpture immediately beneath, which range from simple imagery and leaf forms to full-blown representations of the deceased's character and occupation.

Many old **fonts** were destroyed during the Civil War, and even more in the Commonwealth when they were replaced by pewter or tin basins. At the Restoration many which had been put to secular use were reinstated. The bowl or the stem might have been destroyed in the meantime, so there are several instances of a post-Reformation bowl on an earlier stem and vice versa. But there was none of the Gothic tradition in the design of the seventeenth-century font. The bowl was usually octagonal or hexagonal, and might be made of polished marble. Some had a large diameter, but only a relatively small hollow for the baptismal water, and were generally shallow. Others were chalice-shaped with thick concave stems, or took the form of a shallow bowl on a sturdy Baroque baluster. It became fashionable, especially in the years immediately following the Restoration, to carve the date boldly with perhaps the church warden's initials on one face of the bowl. With few exceptions there was little attempt at much in the way of decoration. Panel work was often quite plain or else included single floral motifs. There might be an upper band or frieze of linked Classical decoration. Some deeper bowls were given round-headed arches. Bases and plinths were usually plain.

Pulpits appeared in English churches in the fifteenth century but were rare until well into the sixteenth century. They were almost universal by the second quarter of the seventeenth century, and were the church's most important piece of furniture after the Reformation. The term 'Jacobean' denotes more a style of woodworking than a defined period since much so-called – especially in the pulpit line – might be Elizabethan or even Carolean. Early pulpits had an hexagonal drum with a top rail and moulded cornice above, a bottom rail and slender stem. The way in which the panels were carved showed its age.

The seventeenth-century pulpit was conspicuously placed in a central position. It had a curved stairway and gracefully turned balustrade, and included a reading desk. The latter might be hinged, as was also a step to give more height to the preacher and allow him to see beyond the rising pews. The pulpit had a carved back piece joined above to an hexagonal tester, an acoustic sounding board

encompassed by a frieze which sometimes included pendants. During the next century these sounding boards became bigger, more highly decorated, and were sometimes placed at roof level.

With the advent of galleries, high and horse-box pews, the three-decker pulpit came about. It had ascending levels, a clerk's desk, a priest's desk or reading pew and the pulpit proper. There might be an almost horizontally rising arrangement or a virtual cluster of woodwork enclosed, and with a door to each section. The panel work was invariably plain in sharp contrast to the Jacobean designs of a few years before. Then there were few spaces left uncarved, although the piece was designed not as individual panels but a symmetrical whole. Arches predominated; there was some figurework but much strapwork, angels' heads, fruit and foliage. Testers were often gilded and included sunflowers and doves. The fixture would have been sumptuously hung with velvet, and cushioned.

From the end of the sixteenth century hour glasses swung on their brackets, attached in a casing of wrought ironwork to either the pulpit or a nearby pillar. They were intended to regulate the time of the sermon, and at least showed the priest when to turn them over and start again.

The focal point of the **Georgian country church** was the two- or three-decker pulpit in oak or deal with tester, perhaps also an hour glass and iron candle holders. It was centrally placed so that the priest, when given the additional height of his footstool, could loom large over his congregation and they could hear him. Below was a collection of plainly panelled, high backed and horsebox pews fitted with doors, hinged and locked to keep out the draughts. They had bookrests, narrow ledged seats and sometimes drawers beneath. The squire might have provided his family with a sumptuous pew in a position where they were the least likely to be disturbed; raised, carpeted, upholstered, and with a fireplace.

Rustic Georgian woodwork could be atrocious; bits and pieces of mediaeval fittings re-made in a piecemeal fashion. Or it might be excellent joinery, and we find the ends of pews skilfully curved around, for example, the font or pillars. Curved and panelled, too, might be the **galleries.** Since the demise of the rood loft one might be the home of the organ or the village band. Galleries were built wherever space permitted, facing the pulpit. Their panels were often inscribed with suitable biblical texts which, in the forms of the Lord's Prayer, Creed and Decalogue also adorned the panels of the altar piece. Elsewhere panels listed benefactors, and local worthies were remembered by the huge ledger stones, great floor slabs containing armorial bearings and details of the deceased.

High on the walls were lozenge-shaped coats of arms called **hatchments,** removed from the outside of the deceased's house after several months. Their design conformed to strict rules. The arms of the deceased were always on a black background; in a union the male to the left, and his wife to the right. The survivor's arms were painted on a white background. Widows and widowers followed the same plan, with diamond and shield shapes respectively which were painted on an all-black background. Spinsters and bachelors had single arms in a lozenge or shield respectively on a black background. The exception to the general rule involved a deceased bishop, whose arms were to the right, next to those of his see. A bishop's wife had perhaps the most elaborate heraldry of all; reverting to the male left, female right rule, we have double arms on each side: the bishop's see and his, his and hers.

The walls of the church were white and light flooded in through the clear glass of the large round-headed windows.

◄119 *Mildenhall, Wiltshire: the nave showing Gothick woodwork (1815–16)*

7
Victorian 1830-1900

It is easy to malign the whole Victorian contribution to church architecture. The result pales in the wake of the inspiration. The planned Gothic revival did not achieve the anticipated success in its time, and many of the architects' unsympathetic approach to restoration does not accord with our own feelings for preservation. At the beginning of the nineteenth century church building, design and materials had recently gone through a frivolous approximation of Gothic. Most people were ignorant of the purely functional origins of church building and little had been done to understand the development of pre-Reformation symbolism. Architects were guilty of insensitivity and intolerant of the quaint if frankly piecemeal way in which successors had patched up their inheritance.

The policy of dealing drastically with this work in fact saved many churches which were in a poor condition, even down to the floors which were uneven and full of pits; some, as may still be seen in small country churches which have been left alone, almost sculptured like waves upon a beach. The debt we owe in this respect must in some measure offset their despoliation under the guise of restoration. It is also true that not all restoration was bad; sufficient funds and a good architect could achieve much. When the Victorians started from scratch their achievement was often of high quality and they worked with a conviction, albeit one which we may feel to have been misplaced. Builders may strive to reproduce the work of another age, but they do so by using their increased knowledge

and experience, if not technology. They cannot recapture the original inspiration born of feelings and factors they themselves could never know. This is why a Victorian church, however well disguised, will always be obviously Victorian.

The influences typical of the Victorian Age began earlier than the nineteenth century, just as much of it was spent well before its end. The period can be divided into Early Victorian (1830–50), High Victorian (1850–70) and Late Victorian (1870–1900).

Gothic was never entirely abandoned, even after the Restoration. It is possible to see the essence of pre-Reformation work done at almost any time. In fact country areas far removed from the centres of taste and learning might anyway be 50 years behind the fashions, and those of a more temporary nature could altogether pass them by.

In 1747 Horace Walpole moved into 'Strawberry Hill', Twickenham and soon began to convert and expand it in a Gothic style which took the name Strawberry Hill and had some influence on architectural taste. From the middle of the eighteenth century Gothic crept back as non-structural work, mostly external. It was used to give what was considered in some quarters to be an ancient and proper 'feel'. But it included moulded plasterwork throughout, high pews and an all important pulpit which were to be despised and removed when the Victorians defined their 'correct' Gothic. In 1765 a stonemason in his father's firm, turned builder, John Carr (1723–1807), who had done some Palladian-style domestic architecture, began to design churches. His work in this field made him one of the earliest of the Gothic revivalists.

There was little church building at the end of the eighteenth century or for the first third of the nineteenth. What there was latterly did not have the charm of earlier Georgian Gothic and there were traces of Perpendicular. Architects like William Porden (1755–1822) were designing Gothic buildings in the provinces. The industrial architect John Dobson (1787–1865) had a long career during which he either designed or rebuilt many churches in the north. Unlike the stricter architects to come he began the nineteenth century by putting up Classical churches, changed to early Gothic with the fashion of its third decade, but still later managed to please the Ecclesiologists with good Decorated work. In contrast was the early work of Henry Hake Seward (1778–1848) who during the second decade of the century built a succession of small, simple Gothic buildings.

Then the effects of the population explosion, the Industrial Revolution, the migration and distribution of the people all contributed towards the need for new churches. It was the locations which had changed. People with sense and ability realised where potential wealth was and made for the industrial centres. Country churches were gradually emptied whilst the towns had a pressing need to accommodate their increasing population. The rigid structure within the Church of England meant that it could not extend its old parochial system to the new centres of population. The clergy had a bad name, the whole system seemed in imminent danger of collapse, and little was being done by the established church to cope with new social conditions. Where the Church of England was absent non-conformity stepped in.

With the evangelical revival of the early nineteenth century came a more subdued style of Strawberry Hill Gothic. At the same time there was a short neo-Romanesque revival, which was to find more favour in the 1840s. Individual architects favoured Greek, Roman and Gothic styles – often in strange combinations. George Dance the Younger (1741–1825) succeeded his father as architect to the City of London in 1768 and rebuilt the interior of St Bartholomew the Less as an octagon within the original walls.

It was about this time that architecture began to develop as a profession and men who made their living from it took on assistants and then pupils. They all worked long hours and those apprenticed might spend a decade or more in learning their craft at home and then by travelling abroad. In this way foreign influences were kept alive in English architecture and a variety of neo-classicism adorned churches at the beginning of the nineteenth century. The general uncertainty which prevailed before 1830 stunted any real development and occasioned many architectural monstrosities. In the provinces many churches were the work of amateur architects, diverse in their approach but moving away from local styles. They produced their own plans and constrained the builder to put together brick and stone as instructed. In a way they helped to make architects a recognised, professional body. This approach of a group of pupils and assistants adopting the styles of the head of their office, gave rise to a more formal general style in the 1860s, when High Victorian Gothic was well established.

In 1803, Parliament passed the Gifts For Churches Acts (amended 1811): 'to promote the building, repairing or otherwise providing of Churches and Chapels, and of Houses for the Residence of Ministers, and the providing of Church Yards and Glebes'. These Acts also provided for 'decent and suitable accommodation for all persons, of what rank or degree soever . . . and whose circumstances may render them unable to pay for such accommodation'. Thinking people whose minds were fresh with the result of the French Revolution, the rise of non-conformity and the pressure for civil and religious rights for such sects, were soon to consider

120 *St Pancras, Euston Road, London
(1819–22) by William and Henry William
Inwood*

alternative religious thought: true Catholic principles or allegiance to dissenting bodies. There were to be no half measures acceptable to the advocates of strict taste in the 1840s and without a spirit of compromise Pugin's conversion to Catholicism lost the Anglican church what might have been its most inspired source of new buildings.

Sir James Hall published his *Essay On The Origin, History and Principles of Gothic Architecture* as early as 1813. Four years later a self-taught Liverpool architect, Thomas Rickman (1776–1841) published *An Attempt To Discriminate The Styles Of English Architecture From The Conquest To The Reformation,* a classification based on the gradual lowering of window arches. His terminology met with opposition, giving an alternative to the prevalent Gothic divisions First, Middle and Third Pointed. Others, particularly Edmund Sharpe, divided Rickman's Decorated into Geometrical and Curvilinear by the appearance of the ogee arch, and substituted Rectilinear for the next period. All of these terms remain in common usuage to describe styles within each of the latter two Gothic periods, but Rickman's terminology was accepted.

A Parliamentary Commission for Building New Churches was set up in 1818 when church architecture was of a very low standard. The State made a grant of one million pounds which was insufficient for all the work which needed to be done, and the churches which resulted were known as 'Commissioners' Churches'. The designs approved by the Church Commissioners were less favoured by the users. They were executed in a Grecian style or in Gothic which was inferior to that of the second half of the preceeding century. Whilst they proved to be a means by which young architects could establish themselves, they were subject to various constraints. The two basic criteria were economy and the need to produce halls which could hold a great many people. Later, various groups of thinkers formulated very definite views on the way in which the design of the church should be approached, and sought to impose it on the architects. The Church Building Society, formed in 1818 and incorporated ten years later, proved to be of great financial assistance in building and repairing Anglican churches.

In 1821 Wyatt's pupil Augustus Charles Pugin (1769–1832) – artist, architectural designer and teacher – published *Specimens of Gothic Architecture* in two volumes. This and other of his publications were amongst the first to feature accurately drawn figures of mediaeval architecture, and inspired his more famous son not only to assist with them but to continue the elder Pugin's work after his death.

One of the earliest architects to obtain the Church Commissioners' patronage was Thomas Rickman, who had been building Georgian neo-Gothic churches since the start of the nineteenth century and continued to do so until c. 1840. He was at his most prolific in the 16 years from the formation of the Commission, working mainly in the midlands and remaining faithful to the Georgian plan. Yet for someone who had an unrivalled knowledge of mediaeval architecture it was odd that he should rarely build his economical churches in one or other of its styles. When he did, he favoured Perpendicular. His contemporary Edward Blore (1787–1879) might have been an even greater influence on the first 50 years of Victorian church architecture. Although also a great mediaevalist, building Decorated and Perpendicular style churches c. 1824–48, he put up Romanesque and Early English buildings.

Strangely England's great classical architect, the then elderly Sir John Soane (1753–1837) built only three Commissioners' Churches, all of little note. As the Commission was being set up the father and son Greek Revivalist office of William and Henry William Inwood was designing St Pancras (1819–22), which proved to be unique and thoroughly Greek in both constructional style and decoration. Their later churches, although in a similar style, were inferior. But it is interesting that such a monument as St Pancras was erected almost at the moment when the scene shifted to Gothic. Some lesser architects such as Peter Atkinson (1776–1843) spent a decade or so almost exclusively designing numerous churches for the Commissioners. He specialised in lancet windows, but his interiors were no less dull than those of his contemporaries.

Another Renaissance revivalist who worked for the Commissioners in the provinces was the widely travelled Sir Charles Barry (1795–1860). After studying extensively throughout Europe and the Mediterranean regions he came back to do a crash course in Commissioners' Gothic of the early 1820s. He worked in this style 1822–46, and was fond of internal galleries and unsympathetic towards the Ecclesiologists' demands for deep chancels separated from the nave by high rood screens. Some of his churches were Italianate, and when strict rules came into being in the 1840s Barry turned his attention to public buildings. A fine Italian Romanesque design was done by Thomas Henry Wyatt (1807–1880) at Wilton, Wiltshire, at a time (1841–5) when it might have been considered in direct conflict with the edicts of the moment. At the same time he too was building to Georgian proportions, in the middle of a long and fruitful career. He was also a considerable restorer of little note.

In the 38 years which followed the Parliamentary Commission there were as many Church Building Acts. Throughout the third decade of the century most new churches had a Gothic feeling, although the Georgian style continued until well into the 1830s. Some early Victorian churches were of Georgian dimensions and symmetry, with Romanesque style structures and decoration. This was followed by a return to thirteenth century architecture, but of a type as might have been influenced by several foreign sources. Amateur architects and others who had little or no experience of church building came straight from secular work, being quick

to realise the potential in the new need which might establish their reputations and their fortunes. Soon the vogue for 'correct' Gothic buildings sorted the amateurs from the professionals or at least those who were prepared to study and build in sympathy with the prevailing thought.

A large number of standard Gothic churches were built in the provinces in the 1820s, 30s and 40s by a host of mainly regional architects who achieved little of real distinction. Some were better known for their domestic architecture and public buildings, and what they turned their hands to in the ecclesiastical line tended to be more stereotyped. These young architects were almost entirely of the nineteenth century. Outside London were such people as William Railton (1801–1877), who favoured Early English; George Webster (1797–1864), who put in a third of a century of church building, restoring, etc., in the north west; and H. J. Underwood (1804–52), who typified the Victorian approach to church building at the time.

From 1833 the leader of the Gothic Revival in England was Augustus Welby Northmore Pugin (1812–52), a brilliant eccentric who was obsessed with the effects of morals on architecture. His values epitomised our own misguided conception of the universal Victorian attitude to religion. But however quaint and confused may be his basic theories to our minds, they were at least born out of Pugin's belief that the better the society, the better the architecture which results. Such a theory obviously has especial significance in the question of church architecture.

The Ecclesiastical Commissioners were established in 1836 and given wide controls over matters of finance and property as well as the ability to pursue sweeping administrative reforms. In the same year Pugin published Contrasts, heavily biased illustrations between what he believed to be the true Gothic as exemplified by Decorated architecture and the prevailing neo-Gothic. He argued that fourteenth-century architecture in England resulted from the Christian faith in its purest form and was therefore the only true Christian style. This strange reasoning established for the Victorians what they for a while accepted as the principles of 'correct' Gothic building. This gave impetus to a programme of building which was every bit as ambitious as that of mediaeval England, even if it lacked its quality.

The Oxford or Tractarian Movement was founded in 1833 under the leadership of John Keble, R. H. Froud, Edward Bouverie Pusey and John Henry Newman. It urged the complete study of theology, ecclesiastical history, liturgy and evangelism, issuing its ideas in a series of printed *Tracts For The Times*. Many of these were opposed by both politicians and churchmen for they sought to elevate the church above the state and re-establish the Church of England with full Catholic doctrine and ritual as a reformed member of the Catholic church. They preached that the allegiance of the Church should be to the form of pre-Reformation worship, doctrine and ecclesiastical history. This occasioned considerable controversy over the respective merits of 'high' and the then common 'low' church approach. For the first time in centuries men were seriously arguing over theology and ritual, the decline of standards within the church and the necessity for a properly ordained priesthood. Many of those ordained as a result were scholar priests of independent means whose private wealth financed much church building and restoration.

In 1839 John Mason Neale and Benjamin Webb formed a group of ecclesiologists in Cambridge called the Camden Society. They took their name from that of William Camden, the scholarly antiquarian and historian who published *Britannia* in 1586 and whose approach laid the foundations for the style of historical research in the seventeenth century. The term 'ecclesiology' was coined to describe the science and study of church art and architecture, furniture, decoration and liturgy. The Camden Society issued a number of pamphlets and although they were fundamentally concerned with religious controversy, their ideas had a marked effect on the church architecture of the 1840s. They thought that churches should be used as they were before the Reformation and that the mediaeval approach to Gothic architecture made it the only true Christian type. But they went even further; they argued that everything has a beginning, middle and end which equates with experiment, maturity and decline, the middle being the most vigorous and pure.

In terms of Rickman's classification this meant that Early English was considered to be the experimental stage, and Perpendicular was decadent. Fourteenth-century Decorated was English Gothic at its best, and this was the style which was imposed on architects from 1845 onwards. Strict rules were drawn up which insisted, amongst other things, that only original materials should be used to build churches, and the work should be done only by architects who were Christians and had apparently impeccable morals.

The Camden Society became the Ecclesiological Society (1846–68). It had never been properly decided at which point Decorated architecture was at its peak, and many churches were built in the late Decorated/early Perpendicular style if sufficient funds were available. Elsewhere Norman or Lombardic-style churches were built in the 1840s, and in small villages these continued to be put up throughout the decade.

The leader of the Gothic Revival was William Butterfield (1814–1900) an uncompromising man and severe Ecclesiologist who nonetheless built in an individual manner and went in for lofty steeples. His work could be angular and austere. He subscribed to the importance of natural materials for construction, and the combination of any natural colours in decoration. In this he was one of the first to use polychromy: differently coloured stones, bricks, marbles, etc., arranged to create an ornate surface pattern. This became one of the main features of High Victorian Gothic. Butterfield eschewed the mediaeval style of wall painting in favour of more permanent structural decoration, so that even the passing of time hardly lessens the harsh effect on the eye. He not only designed buildings, but also the furniture which went into them, and was particularly active in this field for the Camden Society.

Polychromy and garishness went hand in hand. The same minds which approved of pink and grey brick in juxtaposition, black and yellow, red, honey colours and much more of the same nature, also endorsed coloured roofing tiles, highly polished marbles of contrasting hues and the encaustic tile. So taken were the designers with the possibilities afforded by the machines of the Industrial Revolution that they seemed unable to see how ghastly was the result. Not content with polychromatic banding on their own exteriors, the internal decoration which rivalled the mediaeval walls for garishness but without the genuine religious conviction, they also topped ancient buildings with red tiles and set up polished marble against centuries-old stonework.

Perhaps the most famous architect of the period was Sir Gilbert Scott (1810–77), who studied Gothic architecture during the 1830s and built profusely in that style during the next two decades. Nowhere in England is far from a church in which he had at least a hand. By the sheer volume of his work he perhaps did more than any other to popularise the Revival amongst the people, even if he offered little originality and much which was dull. The canal network had opened up the country for the transportation of materials, but Gilbert Scott's career was helped in no small measure by the coming of the railways. In a way they created a need for some churches, like St Mark's, Swindon, in which the communities of railway employees could worship. The Industrial Revolution generally occasioned more, and the work centres of the midlands and north bred their own local architects. But

for Scott there were no boundaries and he built, added and restored throughout the length and breadth of the country. In 1877 William Morris, a trained architect turned painter and poet with a particular liking for Gothic work, founded the Society For The Protection Of Ancient Buildings as a protest against what he considered to be Scott's unnecessary restorations.

Another active Ecclesiologist was Scott's one-time assistant George Edmund Street (1824–81), who paid considerable attention to interior colour and polychromy, and produced his best churches in High Victorian Gothic during the 1860s. Street's practice was large and his influence was wide. It was paralleled by the career of George Frederick Bodley (1827–1907), another pupil of Scott, whose earlier work was simpler Gothic but whose use of colour and materials developed along more sensitive lines than that of his contemporaries. His best work followed Street's, from 1890 to the end of the century.

Many of these architects were influenced by foreign styles and use of materials which the Ecclesiologists had at first been unable to accept. During the 1850s English church architects looked to Italian work, and in 1855 Street published *Brick and Marble Architecture of the Middle Ages in Italy.* But the movement was not sterile, and those who introduced colour into church building came from within its ranks and helped the development towards an English form of Victorian Gothic; men like William Burges (1827–81), who built a number of parish churches like those of thirteenth century France. This style was more solid and simple than its Early English counterpart, and the Victorian revival followed the vogue for Decorated during the third quarter of the century. By the 1880s architects had returned to copy English work of the thirteenth, fourteenth and fifteenth centuries.

121 *St Mark's, Swindon, Wiltshire (1843–5) by George Gilbert Scott and W. B. Moffatt*

122 *St Giles, Camberwell by George Gilbert Scott*

123 *Church of the Holy Innocents, Higham, Gloucestershire (1847–51): Henry Woodyer, architect; wall paintings by Thomas Gambier-Parry*

124 *St Cuthbert's, Philbeach Gardens, London (1884–7)*

Some of the best Victorian churches came from John Loughborough Pearson (1817–97), who was to crown his career with Truro Cathedral (from 1879), built in the French style of the thirteenth century. His churches were large and high and he mostly remained faithful to the thirteenth century, doing his best work mainly in the suburbs of London. Although highly competent and in his own practice whilst yet in his twenties, Pearson's first church to impress was not started until 1849 and it was after c. 1860 that his work reached a sustained peak of excellence. Most of these churches contain beautiful stone vaults with brickwork between the ribs, and in one the vaulting is entirely of stone.

The Ecclesiologists had the chance to make an immediate impact. By the 1840s many churches had fallen into decay. Instead of trying to preserve work which was less rigid and boring than their own, they preferred to clear out the alterations, fixtures and fittings of the two preceding centuries and substitute their 'correct' imitations. Their churches were to be arranged like those of the fourteenth century, bearing in mind the style of worship as set out in the Prayer Book of 1662.

The auditory **plan** and the type of furniture within it displeased the Ecclesiologists. Not that architects ever returned to an arrangement of chapels and side altars. Although galleries were sometimes put into new churches of the 1840s, many an awkwardly sited example came down, admitting light and space between the arches of the nave arcade. The nave and chancel might be a separated by a screen or steps and the latter increased in size to accommodate facing stalls for the priest and choir before a raised altar, itself contained in a sanctuary behind low altar rails. Decayed piscina and sedilia were repaired. The altar was once more the focal point of worship, set in a highly decorated chancel. All seating in the nave was arranged to face it. As galleries were removed, the organ was set up close to the chancel, if not on its north wall where it was conveniently situated for the choir. There was a revival in the polygonal apse, and some chancels were vaulted. To begin with, the renewed importance attached to chancels meant that new ones were built larger, and indeed the walls of a Victorian Gothic church tended to be higher than in the corresponding mediaeval period. By the 1880s the dominant feature was once more the nave.

The nave lost its high furniture and seating was low, open and uncomfortable so that people could give their attention to the matters in hand. The central, three-decker pulpit was demolished and its place taken by a smaller, lower structure situated on the north side of the chancel steps. Many of the neo-Gothic stone examples are heavy, overpowering and in poor taste. Opposite, on the south side of the steps was the lectern or book rest, commonly made of brass or wood in the form of an eagle with spread wings. The Victorians placed their **fonts** centrally at the west end. Square and circular bowls were favoured, usually with a heavy central stem and four shafts which might or might not be constructional. The shafts with their bases and caps, plinths and – in many cases – the bowls were of highly polished marble. Sometimes the bowls were decorated like an inlaid kaleidoscope, others had texts around the rim. Rarely are they any more tastefully done than Victorian pulpits.

Low ceilings were thrown across the church, hiding the beams which – in many cases – fairly recent Georgian work had revealed. Since imagery no longer offended the authorities wall paintings appeared once more; so too repeated, painted devices around columns and capitals, over nave arcades and on expanses of blank wall. Tendrils, vines, leaves and flowers were employed in this way, although flatly done.

The demand for church building had now far exceeded the supply of people available to do the work. The needs supplied by the new centres of population as a result of the Industrial Revolution were in some ways being satisfied by the machinery itself, producing new materials for new churches.

Victorian craftsmen had already once started from scratch when they took on Gothic without the years of evolution to back their work. Soon they were to create textures and designs which were unknown to the Gothic craftsman, and colouring which he had been unable to produce. Really, they were creating Gothic using their own materials; continuing the Middle Ages as if nothing had happened in between.

In 1856 the Church Building Commissioners relinquished their power to the Ecclesiastical Commissioners, who were then 21 years old. Three years later the English Church Union – originally and briefly called the Church of England Protection Society – was founded to promote Catholic practices and High Church principles within the Church of England. It had become apparent that there was going to be a distinct High and Low Church split within Victorian Gothic of the 1860s. Both terms had long been in use; 'High Church' was first used at the end of the seventeenth century and 'Low Church' from early in the eighteenth, now revived.

The beliefs of the latter, more usually connected with those of the Protestant nonconformists, gave little credence to exalted claims for the sacraments and those who administered them. The churches were more secular in character and much plainer than their counterparts. On the other hand, some high churchman who adopted Tractarian principles introduced considerable ceremonial into their services. These were the highly decorated buildings. A priesthood which promoted the importance of Catholic Christianity and ritual with the Church of England was supported in its views by influential patrons and architects.

In *An Analysis of Gothick Architecture* (1860) Raphael and J. Arthur Brandon warned that 'Undue importance must not be attached to the terms Early, Decorated and Perpendicular Gothic, as though they denoted so many distinct styles in Church Architecture.'

Whilst the Victorians were able to copy mediaeval styles they could not express their faith in quite the same physical terms as their predecessors, whose lofty towers were put up to the glory of God, dominating all around them. Building regulations were changed in the 1860s, allowing Victorian office blocks to rise above church towers in the towns. In London it meant the end of Christopher Wren's carefully planned skyline where all towers drew the eye to St Pauls. The great strength of the time was not primarily in architectural style but in religious doctrine. This provided the impetus for High Victorian Gothic, not only in structural work but also in decorative art. The movement was led and inspired by William Morris and the painter Edward Coley Burne-Jones, great friends who had both been influenced by Rossetti.

Morris was particularly concerned with the effects of mechanisation on the craftsman whose prices were being undercut at the expense of individuality. He wanted craftsmen to be given status similar to that of their pre-Reformation counterparts, but failed because machinery could mass produce items quickly and more cheaply.

Stained glass particularly benefited and some fine work was done from the 1850s in marked contrast to the dull and dim windows which were heavily religious but allowed little light to permeate the general gloom. Now there was a great revival in stained glass, although it did not achieve the vivid depth of colour of its fourteenth-century best or the lighter tones of the fifteenth century. Like so much, it had to be learnt afresh and its exponents were also influenced by the Romantic and artistic movements of the day, particularly the pre-Raphaelites.

Late Victorian architects took more of an interest in all aspects of their churches than ever before. They were freed from the strict Decorated work, and some returned to the Italianate style. Perpendicular once more became popular and tall, narrow arches appeared. Within this general framework artists of the day created furnishings and decorations.

INDEX

Index

abaci 21, 35, 53, 66
alternate billet 25, 30
ambulatory 21
Ancient Buildings, Society for the Protection
  of 108
angle buttresses 61
Anglo-Saxon 11-22
annulets 53
apses 12, 25, 113
arcading 29, 45
arch-braced roof 62
arch construction 52
arches 21, 35, 40, 52, 68, 84, 98
Atkinson, Peter 106
auditory plan 94
aumbry 15
Aylesbury fonts 38

ball-flower 58, 65, 68
balusters 19, 20, 21, 94
bar tracery 51, 64
Baroque (defined) 87
barrel roof 74
barrel vault 31, 79
Barry, Sir Charles 106
bases 21, 35, 53, 68, 85
basilican plan 11, 12-13, 21
battlements 73-74
bead decoration 25, 30, 35
beak heads 26-27, 31
belfry openings 19, 63, 81
bell-cotes 45
Benedictine order 40
billet decoration 25
Biscop, Benedict 18
Black Death (effects of) 56
Blore, Edward 105
Bodley, George Frederick 108
Bodmin fonts 39
Book of Common Prayer 89
bosses 62, 79
bowtell moulding 43
Brandon, Raphael and J. Arthur 114
broach spires 48-49, 63-64
building materials 16

Burges, William 108
Burne-Jones, Edward Coley 114
Butterfield, William 107-108
buttresses 28, 45, 46, 60-61, 64, 74, 96

cable moulding 26, 30, 35
Camden Society 107
capitals 35, 53
Carr, John 102-103
cartouches 99
Celtic plan 12
chamfer stops 44-45
chamfers 28, 35, 60
chancels 12, 43, 57
chevron 25, 30
church art 15, 21
Church Building Commissioners 114
Church Building Society 105
churchyard crosses 14
circular windows 32, 64, 65
Cistercian order 40
Classical architecture 87-101
Classical orders 87
clerestory 25, 57, 62-63, 76-77
collar beam 62
colour in churches 81-83
Commissioners' churches 105, 106
composite order 88
corbels 29
Corinthian order 87-88
cornices 95
craftsmanship 56
crockets 44, 58, 68
Cromwell, Thomas 89
cross shafts, use of 22
cruciform churches 25
crypts 21
curvilinear tracery 64, 65
cusps 49, 51

dagger decoration 64
Dance, George the Younger 103
Decorated architecture 56-69
decorative motifs 14-15, 22, 25-28, 32, 33,
  53-54, 66, 68, 72

Devil's door   33
diagonal buttresses   61
Dobson, John   103
dog tooth   44
Dominican order 42
Doric order   87
doors   33, 35, 66, 84
doorways   20-21, 32-33, 52, 66, 84, 98
double cone decoration   25, 30
double hammerbeam roof   75
double saddleback roof   31
dripstones   50-51, 72-73

easter sepulchres   68
early Christian art   14-16
Early English architecture   42-55
Ecclesiastical Commissioners   106, 144
Ecclesiological Society   107
Ecclesiologists   106, 113
Elizabethan architecture (defined)   87
embattled decoration   26, 30
entablature   87

façades   57
fan vaulting   74-76, 79
Feock fonts   39
flamboyant tracery   65
flowing tracery   65
flushwork 83-84
flying buttresses   46, 64
foils   49, 63, 64
fonts   21-22, 37-39, 54-55, 69, 85-86, 99,113
four-petalled flower   58
Froud, R. H.   107

gable crosses   52
galleries   101
gargoyles   48
geometrical tracery   64
Georgian architecture (defined)   87
Georgian country church   101
Georgian Gothic   95
Gifts for Churches Acts   103
glasswork   18, 49, 56, 65, 76-77, 81
Gothic revival   107
groined vault   31, 79
ground plans   13, 24, 42-43, 57, 71, 92, 113

Hall, Sir James   105
hammerbeam roof   75
hatchments   101
Hawksmoor, Nicholas   93
Hereford fonts   38
herringboning   16
horseshoe arch   35

indented decoration   25
interlacing   30

Inwood, W. and H. W.   105
Ionic order   87
intersecting tracery   64

Jacobean work (defined)   87
Jones, Inigo   87, 90

Keble, John   107
Kentish tracery   65
key decoration   30
knotwork   30

label stops   72-73
lady chapels   42
lancet windows   49-50
Laud, William   89
Launceston fonts   39
leaf decoration   30, 35, 53, 68
lierne ribs   62, 75
lierne vault   79
long and short work   17
lozenge decoration   25, 30

masons 13-14, 16, 42
medallion decoration   26, 30
Mediaeval architecture, Victorian
   classification   105
Morris, William   108, 114
monuments   98-99
mouchette   65
mouldings   25-27, 32, 33, 35-36, 38, 40-41,
   43-45, 53-55, 58, 60, 61, 65, 88, 93-94, 95

nail-head decoration   26, 30, 65
nave towers   17, 18, 31
Neale, John Mason   107
neo-Romanesque revival   103
Newman, John Henry   107
Norfolk fonts   39
Norman architecture   23-39

ogee design   60, 65, 66, 69
ornamentation   14-15, 22, 25-28, 32, 33, 53-54,
   66, 68, 72, 88, 93-94, 95, 98
Oxford Movement   107

Palladian (defined)   87
parapets   48, 63, 73, 79, 81, 97
parclose screens   86
Parliamentary Commission for Building New
   Churches   105
Pearson, John Loughborough   113
pediments   93
pellet decoration   25, 30
Perpendicular architecture   70-86
piers   21, 35, 52-53, 66, 84
pilaster strips   17, 96
Pillar and Portico era   93-94

pillar piscina   37
piscinas   15, 37, 54, 68
plaintain leaf   41
plait decoration   30
plasterwork   95-96
plate tracery   51
plinths   36, 37, 54, 68, 85
pointed arch   40, 43, 47-48
polychromy   107-108
porches   51-52, 66, 83-84, 97-98
Porden, William   103
porticos   93
porticus   18
pulpits   99, 101
Pugin, Augustus Charles   105
Pugin, Augustus Welby Northmore   106-107
Purbeck marble   41
Puritans   89
Pusey, Edward Bouverie   107

quadripartite vaults   31, 79
quoining   16

Railton, William   106
rectilinear tracery   81
Renaissance architecture   87-101
reticulated tracery   65
rib work   47
ribbed vault   79
Rickman, Thomas   105
Roman basilica   11
rood lofts   86
roofs   29-30, 47, 61-62, 72, 74-75, 76, 95-96
round-headed arch   40

saddleback roofs   31
scalloping   30, 35
Scott, Sir Gilbert   108
screens   86
scroll moulding   44
sedilia   37, 54, 68
segmental arch   52
seven sacraments fonts   86
Seward, Henry Hake   103
sexpartite vaults   31
six-lobed flower   30
Soane, Sir John   105
spiral decoration   35
spires   31, 48, 49, 63, 92-93
spur moulding   35, 38
squinches   49
stained glass   114
stair turrets   31, 48, 63, 77
star decoration   26, 30
steeples   63, 97

stiff leaf   40-41, 44, 53
stilted arch   35
Strawberry Hill   102
Street, George Edmund   108
string courses   17, 28-29, 46-47, 61
Supremacy, Act of   88
Sussex fonts   39

three-celled plan   25
three-gabled arrangement   71
tie beams   29, 61-62
tombs   98-99
tongue moulding   35
Torrigiani, Pietro   88
Tournai marble   39
towers   17-18, 25, 47-48, 63, 77, 79, 81, 92-93, 97
tracery   51, 64-66
Tractarian movement   107
transepts   25, 43
Transitional architecture   40-41
trefoil-headed arch   52
triforia   25, 57
two-celled plan   12, 25

Underwood, H. J.   106

Valor Ecclesiasticus   89
vaulting   31, 43, 47, 62, 75, 79
Victorian architecture   102-114
vine scroll   14
Vitruvius   87
volute   30, 35

wagon roofs   74
wall memorials   99
walls   12, 16-17, 28, 41, 45, 60, 73-74, 95
Walpole, Horace   102
waterhold   53-54, 55
waterleaf   30, 41
wave moulding   58
Webb, Benjamin   107
Webster, George   106
wheel windows   32, 65
windows   18-19, 31-32, 41, 49-51, 64-66, 76-77, 81, 96
woodwork   99, 101
Wren, Age of   87
Wren, Sir Christopher   90
Wren's London churches   90, 92
Wyatt, Thomas Henry   106

'Y'-tracery   64

zig-zag   25, 30, 35